THE GUIDE TO WRITING
FANTASY AND SCIENCE FICTION

6 Steps to Writing and Publishing Your Bestseller!

PHILIP ATHANS

Introduction and Original Story by R. A. Salvatore

Aadams media

Avon, Massachusetts

Published by
Adams Media, a division of F+W Media, Inc.
57 Littlefield Street, Avon, MA 02322. U.S.A.
www.adamsmedia.com

ISBN 10: 1-4405-0145-9
ISBN 13: 978-1-4405-0145-6
eISBN 10: 1-4405-0729-5
eISBN 13: 978-1-4405-0729-8

Printed in the United States of America.

10 9 8 7 6 5 4 3 2 1

Library of Congress Cataloging-in-Publication Data
is available from the publisher.

This publication is designed to provide accurate and authoritative information with
regard to the subject matter covered. It is sold with the understanding that the publisher is not engaged in rendering legal, accounting, or other professional advice. If
legal advice or other expert assistance is required, the services of a competent professional person should be sought.
—From a *Declaration of Principles* jointly adopted by a Committee of the
American Bar Association and a Committee of Publishers and Associations

Many of the designations used by manufacturers and sellers to distinguish their product are claimed as trademarks. Where those designations appear in this book and
Adams Media was aware of a trademark claim, the designations have been printed
with initial capital letters.

This book is available at quantity discounts for bulk purchases.
For information, please call 1-800-289-0963.

CONTENTS

INTRODUCTION
WHY FANTASY?

BY R. A. SALVATORE

I'm often asked that question. In fact, at one of my first convention appearances, way back in the early 1990s, a fellow asked me if I was ever going to write "a real book." I didn't laugh then, but I do now.

I've got to backtrack here and explain how I got into writing (and reading). When I was very young, I loved to make up stories, any stories, and I loved to read. I have an amazing collection of "Peanuts" books from the early 1960s. I had a deal with my mom: as long as I was getting straight As, she'd let me bag school occasionally and stay up in my room with my books.

But then something happened. As I went through school, the continual barrage of uninteresting, irrelevant (to me) and tedious reading I was assigned beat the joy of reading right out of me. You might argue with me now about whether *Silas Marner* or *Ethan Frome* are great books, but when I was in the eighth grade, they weren't. Just thinking about them makes my skin crawl to this day.

My aversion to all things reading and writing got so bad that I went to college as a math/computer science major. My freshman year changed all that. For Christmas 1977, my sister Susan gave me a slip-covered four-book set: *The Hobbit* and the three volumes of The Lord of the Rings by J. R. R. Tolkien.

I wasn't happy. I wanted money.

I tossed the books aside and forgot about them, but less than two months later New England got hit by the "Blizzard of '78" (yes, it's in quotes, and if you live in New England, you understand). My college was shut down for a week. I was nineteen and trapped at my mom's house—or so I thought.

Out of complete boredom, I picked up those books. I opened *The Hobbit* to an introduction by a writer named Peter S. Beagle.

"In terms of passwords, the sixties were the time when the word *progress* lost its ancient holiness, an *escape* stopped being comically obscene . . . lovers of Middle-earth want to go there. I would myself, like a shot.

" . . . I once said that the world [Tolkien] charts was there long before him, and I still believe it. He is a great enough magician to tap our most common nightmares, daydreams and twilight fancies, but he never invented them either: he found them a place to live . . . . Let us at last praise the colonizers of dreams."

It's a one-page intro. Three fat paragraphs, but I thought to myself, *now, that was intriguing.* Then I started reading the book, and I didn't stop. I've never stopped. In that one week, I read the four books at least three times. I kept saying aloud, "Why didn't anyone give me this to read in the eighth grade instead of *Silas Marner*?" And I remembered! I remembered those times in my bedroom when I was a kid, alone with my books and my imagination. I remembered a hero building a rocket out of scraps from the back alley and flying it to the moon. I remembered the talking rabbits of *Watership Down* and the friends from *The Wind in the Willows.*

I changed my major so that all of my electives could be literature courses. I discovered Shakespeare and Chaucer and Dante and Twain, but I always kept a soft spot in my heart for J. R. R. Tolkien, who reminded me of the simple joy of twilight fancies, of imagination. So when I decided to write a book after graduation, I naturally went first to fantasy. Maybe it was something as simple as wanting to write a tribute to Tolkien. Partially, at least, it was because there weren't many fantasy books on the shelves in 1982 and I had read all I could find and wanted more, even one of my own. What I didn't realize then, in fact, what took me many years to come to appreciate was that writing in this wonderful genre would become for me a lifelong journey of personal exploration and revelation.

Perhaps more than any other genre, fantasy is about the hero's journey. In a world of seven billion people, with wars I can't stop and legislation I can't even read, the idea of one person being able to make a difference, the idea of one man or woman grabbing a sword and defeating the dragon and saving the village is quite appealing.

And then there is the magic. Magic is faith, and faith is magic. Why did we all feel betrayed in Star Wars Episode 1: *The Phantom Menace*, when Lucasfilm introduced the word *midiochlorian* to explain the Force? Because it demystified the Force, that's why. Because it took the Divine and made it mundane.

In a world whose mysteries are being unraveled by science, it's often easy for the spiritual to be explained away into the secular. It's the way of things, and a good way, I think. But at the same time, as a rational, thinking creature who sees a beginning, a middle, and an end to this existence, I want more. I love the idea of something science can't explain, for that allows me the very human hope that there is something more than this one existence. I want to believe in magic.

In my writing through the decades, I've followed heroes on this same journey, trying to make sense of their winding and surprising road, trying to do what's right and just, even when it's most difficult. The trappings of a fantasy setting allow me to walk the hero's journey, physically and spiritually, to examine the role of a god or gods without tapping the prejudices of real religions, to crystallize the responsibilities to self and community in the face of fantastical danger, and to play with themes of our own world, like racism and sexism, in a safe enough environment to allow both the reader and this writer to let down our natural defensiveness regarding our own foibles and look at the issues honestly.

Because in fantasy perhaps more than in any other genre, the character is rewarded for making the right choices and punished for making the bad.

Ask Boromir.

R. A. Salvatore
January 12, 2010

Welcome to The Guide to Writing Fantasy and Science Fiction

*"Fantasy is the endless optimism that one
person can make a difference."*

—R. A. SALVATORE, creator of The Legend of Drizzt

I can't really remember my first encounter with either fantasy or science fiction. Most likely I had, as a newborn infant, some kind of funny little stuffed unicorn or pacifier in the shape of a turtle smoking a cigar (I was born in 1964, when they used to make stuff like that). Either of those are products of fantasy. Science fiction was likewise everywhere in the early 1960s, when the United States and the Soviet Union were deep into the Space Race. Growing up in the sixties and seventies, I watched a lot of TV, especially science fiction and fantasy shows like *Star Trek, The Banana Splits, Space Ghost,* and *Lost in Space,* and old movies like *Forbidden Planet* and *The Amazing Colossal Man,* which ran on Saturdays on the fuzzy UHF channels.

Today fantasy and science fiction is everywhere, spread across all media from television to the movies to novels and short stories. I'm willing to bet that, like me, you've read J. R. R. Tolkien and/or J. K. Rowling—or Isaac Asimov and/or William Gibson—and said, "I want to do that." You want to be a writer.

I remember writing "books" as soon as I was literate: little pencil-and-crayon affairs lovingly crafted using whatever scraps of paper I could fold. One was called *Red vs. Black,* because I had a red ballpoint pen and a black ballpoint pen, and it just made sense to me that stick figures drawn with one would be the natural enemies of stick figures drawn with the other. My mother gave what we thought was the full collection to my second-grade teacher, who thought I was mentally disabled. (I wasn't disabled—I was shy—and my books were meant to prove that I wasn't "special.") Then the teacher lost 'em. I would give her life to have them back now. A scant few survived, recently discovered in a box in the garage, including my Godzilla knockoff, *Giszingo*; *The $10,000,000 Man*; and the comic book epic *Dizes Dager* (featured on my blog: *http://fantasyhandbook.wordpress.com/2009/12/15/dizes-dager/*).

All of my early works were science fiction stories. Then one day I read a copy of the Marvel Comics Conan adaptations. Though I don't remember exactly how old I was, I sure remember that comic book. I still have it, now lovingly stored in plastic with an acid-free backing, in a box with the rest of my comic book collection, in a corner of my closet where my kids can't touch them until they're old enough to take care of them. In other words, forty.

From there I went on to read the original Robert E. Howard Conan stories, then Edgar Rice Burroughs's John Carter of Mars series, and on and on. I was equally hooked on fantasy and science fiction, thanks to the television series *Lost in Space* and a book that actually made me cry, *The Runaway Robot* by Lester del Rey. When I read a short story by Harlan Ellison called "I Have No Mouth and I Must Scream," I said, "I want to do that." Not in the *Red vs. Black* sense. I wanted to do *that*.

A LITTLE HELP FROM MY FRIENDS

As an editor and author of fantasy novels, I have one of the greatest jobs in the world. This book is my way of letting you in on some of the things I've learned along the way. I also contacted some friends and associates—authors, agents, editors, and others—who lent their time to answer e-mailed questions and add their voices, experience, and advice to this book.

The Guide to Writing Fantasy and Science Fiction isn't meant to cover every bit of the writing process. There are plenty of books on things like grammar and usage, finding an agent, reading a book contract, and so on, so I'm not going to waste lots of space on that stuff. Instead I'll provide advice from someone who's "been there," and been there for a while now.

Let's start at the beginning.

PART I
THE GENRES

"Personally, I don't prefer one kind of fantasy over another. All I care about is the execution."

—PAUL WITCOVER, author of *Waking Beauty* and *Everland*

What is *fantasy*, and what is *science fiction*?

It could be that if you ask a hundred different people you'd get a hundred different answers, but in basic terms, *fantasy* is fiction that depends on magical or supernatural elements not specifically meant to scare you—if it scares you, at least as its primary goal, it's *horror*. If the magical elements are replaced with imagined technologies, it's *science fiction*.

But broad definitions aren't always good enough, so let's get more specific.

CHAPTER 1
WHAT IS FANTASY?

Fantasy fans, authors, critics, and editors alike will argue, sometimes heatedly, over the definitions of the various subgenres of fantasy, but for our purpose, here are mine.

EPIC FANTASY

This is the foundation on which the modern fantasy genre is based. J. R. R. Tolkien's The Lord of the Rings trilogy is the center around which all later epic fantasies have been built. Epic fantasies are huge in scope, most of them are long—more than 100,000 words—and they deal with the biggest possible issues within the novel's milieu. Think of Robert Jordan's The Wheel of Time series or Terry Goodkind's The Sword of Truth. In epic fantasies, a band of heroes will gather to do nothing less than save the world, rescue an entire universe from millennia of darkness, fight the final battle between good and evil, topple empires, and face off against the gods themselves—all against the background of a richly realized world that is entirely the product of the author's imagination.

HIGH FANTASY

High fantasy and epic fantasy are often synonymous in the minds of most fans, and they're closely related. The same care and detail that goes into the world building for an epic fantasy setting will usually appear in high fantasy as well, but what makes high fantasy a little different is the scope of the story. High fantasy tales are more personal than epic fantasies, more limited to the needs and desires of an individual hero. The protagonist is focused on a single villain with personal goals of his own, rather than on some world-shattering cataclysm. Often, at the end of the story, the hero has achieved his goals, but the bigger world goes on largely unaltered. Ursula K. Le Guin's Earthsea novels and Robert Silverberg's Majipoor series fit into the high fantasy subgenre.

SWORD AND SORCERY

These are tales of even smaller scope, with fewer words spent on world building and more spent on action. It wouldn't be out of order to credit Robert E. Howard with the creation of sword and sorcery in his classic tales of Conan, Kull, and others. These are the stories of axe-swinging barbarians splitting their monstrous enemies in twain. Blood is liberally spilled, heads are lopped off here and there, and sexy femmes fatales always need rescuing and are often less than chaste in the way they show their appreciation. This is fantasy for guys. I like to call it "results-oriented" fiction: there's the bad guy, and when he's killed, the story is over.

DARK FANTASY

Dark fantasy should not be confused with horror, because dark fantasy isn't necessarily scary. Rather, it is defined by its approach. In a dark fantasy story, the heroes may not win. In fact, they may not be traditional heroes at all, but antiheroes: people who are morally and ethically ambiguous. The world building is equally dark—the stories are set where evil has triumphed over good, survival of the fittest reigns, and virtue is not necessarily its own reward. H. P. Lovecraft is as well known as an author of dark fantasy as he is an author of traditional horror. Stephen King's The Dark Tower series is a good example as well.

CONTEMPORARY FANTASY

Some call this *urban fantasy*, and it freely intermingles with the horror genre, liberally trading situations and monsters (especially vampires and werewolves), but contemporary fantasy, unlike horror, is not meant to scare you. Though the story depends on magic and supernatural elements, it's set in the "real" world, our Earth, maybe even the city you live in, and in the present day, or close enough that it won't be pegged as either science fiction or historical fantasy. Jim Butcher's popular Dresden Files series is a successful example of contemporary/urban fantasy.

HISTORICAL FANTASY

Like contemporary fantasy, historical fantasy has a solid grounding in the real world, but a real world of years or centuries past. The entire history of the world is open to authors of historical fantasy. Popular fantasy novels have been set everywhere and everywhen, from Victorian England or Civil War America to feudal Japan or Classical Greece. Susanna Clarke's seminal *Jonathan Strange & Mr. Norrell* has become the gold standard for historical fantasies.

EROTIC FANTASY

Likewise growing in popularity, this subgenre is often referred to as *fantasy romance*. Though any of the subgenres not only can but should include some romantic elements, erotic fantasy dials the heat up a few notches—sometimes more than a few. I would define it as a fantasy story in which sex and/or romance are the primary movers for the plot. How "hot" an erotic fantasy novel can get is up to the sensibilities of the author and editor. From the beginning of the romance genre, there have been fantasy elements, such as the ghost in Emily Bronte's *Wuthering Heights*. However, it was Anne Rice who broke this subgenre into the mainstream with the Sleeping Beauty novels she wrote under the pseudonym A. N. Roquelaure.

IN THE WINGS

And . . . ? I think every fantasy fan out there is waiting for someone to show us a new fantasy subgenre. "From a sales perspective," says Kuo-Yu Liang, Vice President of Sales and Marketing for Diamond Book Distributors, "I've seen no difference (in sales of one subgenre over another). It's all about whether the reader is emotionally connected." Chances are that a new subgenre will come from a crossover, or intermingling, of the fantasy genre with other genres.

Though the fantasy genre is largely defined by its archetypes, there's no reason an author should feel limited by them. When an author combines those archetypes with the archetypes of other genres, the fusion can create extraordinary results, bringing about new, as-yet-unnamed subgenres.

If the detective in what would otherwise be a mystery story is a wizard, the mystery becomes a fantasy. If the heroine of a romance novel is a dragon in the guise of a princess, the romance becomes a fantasy. And on and on. However, you need to have equal respect for both (or all three, or all four) genres that you're mixing.

In any case, tell your story. You'll either be missing the trend, riding the trend, or creating the trend. "All of publishing is trend-driven, never mind fantasy," John Betancourt, bestselling author, editor, and publisher of Wildside Press, told me. "It can't be avoided." He's absolutely right.

CHAPTER 2

WHAT IS SCIENCE FICTION?

It's helpful to look at science fiction as a ratio of science to fiction. With a few exceptions, what separates the science fiction subgenres are the proportions of this ratio.

HARD SCIENCE FICTION

This genre is most heavily weighted to the science side. Hard science fiction authors make a careful study of trends in research and technology across broad categories, from astrophysics to biotechnology, and do their best to get right as many of the facts that underlie their imagined technology as they can. Every generation since Jules Verne has had its hard science fiction writers, but Isaac Asimov and Arthur C. Clarke are among the most notable. Current practitioners of the research-intensive art of hard science fiction include Charles Stross and Greg Bear.

MILITARY SCIENCE FICTION

Military science fiction emphasizes warfare in the future, with tales of rugged soldiers bristling with high-tech weaponry, fighting dangerous—usually alien—opponents across the exotic landscapes of distant worlds, or in fleets of starships. Robert A. Heinlein's *Starship Troopers* is a primary text for the military science fiction subgenre, and David Drake, as well as David Weber and his stories of the Honorverse, are Heinlein's heirs apparent. How the author decides to weight that science-to-fiction ratio is optional, but most military science fiction tends to be heavy on the science, though it takes the form of military technology and strategy.

SPACE OPERA

This subgenre has elements of both hard and military science fiction but is defined by a ratio much more heavily weighted to the fiction side. Authors of space opera, from George Lucas to Simon R. Green, are less concerned with how the ray gun works than how cool the hero looks shooting it. Space opera is more fun, though on an intellectual level it's less educational. But never discount its power to energize an audience (case in point: Star Wars).

SLIPSTREAM

Slipstream is the most difficult to define of the science fiction subgenres. Imagine that science fiction ratio so tipped to one side that it's nearly zero percent science, one hundred percent fiction. That raises the obvious question: What makes it *science* fiction? There's no clear answer. Slipstream, a term first coined by author Bruce Sterling, is a cross of science fiction and contemporary fantasy. It's not quite horror—it's not meant to scare you—and it's not about the gadgets and gizmos, but then neither is it inhabited by dragons and elves. I'd put many of the classic stories of Harlan Ellison, such as "Shattered Like a Glass Goblin" and " 'Repent, Harlequin!' Said the Ticktockman" in this category, and Kelly Link is a contemporary darling of the slipstream world. The story "Hugo Mann's Perfect Soul" by R. A. Salvatore at the back of this book is as much a slipstream story as it is a work of contemporary fantasy.

CYBERPUNK

This genre has fallen out of favor of late, if for no other reason than we're now living in the future that its creators first imagined. Cyberpunk concentrates on the future of information/computing technology and the interaction of humanity and machines. William Gibson first coined the term *cyberspace* in the cyberpunk short story "Burning Chrome," and went on to write his masterpiece, *Neuromancer*, which immediately took its place as a classic of the genre.

STEAMPUNK

Steampunk is gaining in popularity in both the adult and young reader arenas. In an article in *Time* magazine, Lev Grossman said of steampunk, "The same way punk took back music, steampunk reclaims technology for the masses. It substitutes metal gears for silicon, pneumatic tubes for 3G and wi-fi. It maximizes what was miniaturized and makes visible what was hidden." Steampunk novelists like Cherie Priest and Jay Lake imagine a world of Victorian-styled technology and science to create a very specific form of historical science fiction.

ALTERNATE HISTORY

Alternate history shares some of steampunk's thinking, but where steampunk is weighted more toward fiction, alternate history is concerned more with real science and real history—with a twist. Alternate history authors like Harry Turtledove take historical research very seriously then imagine "what if" situations, such as: What if Hitler invented the A-bomb before the Americans did? What if the Ancient Egyptians made contact with technologically advanced aliens? Think of alternate history as science fiction's answer to historical fantasy, but with a wider historical scope than is found in steampunk.

SUB-AUIDENCES

Though science fiction fans are generally willing to pass between the different sub-genres, some of these end up with very specific audiences. Military science fiction, for instance, tends to have a predominantly male audience, and there are precious few if any examples of military science fiction written for young readers. But maybe that just means we're waiting for the first great military science fiction series for kids.

In any case, no matter which genre or sub-genre you write in, you must above all have your audience in mind when you start to write. Let's figure out how to do that.

CHAPTER 3
KNOW YOUR AUDIENCE

Fantasy and science fiction appeal to a wide variety of readers and can range from simple chapter books for early readers up to epic series for a sophisticated adult audience. Before getting started on your novel you'll need to decide who you want to write for. Each of the following broad categories, based on reading level, presents its own challenges and will have a significant effect on the story you tell, not just how you tell it. Still, almost all of the subgenres and crossovers we've discussed in the previous chapters can be expressed at any reading level and for any audience.

ADULT, TEEN, AND MIDDLE GRADE

The primary distinction between adult, teen, and middle grade novels is the age of the protagonist. In general, adults like to read about adults, and teens (and tweens) like to read about teens.

Adult Fantasy and Science Fiction

The audience for adult fantasy and science fiction allows greater leeway with elements like sex and violence, but beyond that obvious distinction, adult fantasy tends to have a more sophisticated point of view. You'll want to explore headier subject matter and have a more complex view of politics and relationships. The theme or message of an adult fantasy novel may push boundaries that a children's book couldn't even approach.

Teen Fantasy and Science Fiction

Teen fiction is a rapidly expanding category in all the major bookstores. Though teenagers are particularly subject to distraction from new media such as video games and the Internet, teens do read. Teenage girls seem to read more than boys do, according to most of the industry surveys, but teen boys are particularly drawn to fantasy and science fiction. Teen boys make up a substantial segment of the audience for tie-in fantasy—novels based on role-playing games, video games, and so on—but will pick up original stories as well. Though it may seem old-fashioned to draw distinctions between genders, teen girls tend to be more drawn to character-driven stories with some romance, while boys are a bit more interested in action and adventure.

Middle Grade Fantasy and Science Fiction

Middle grade books are intended for kids ages eight to twelve (third to sixth graders), also known as "tweens." These kids are starting to read on their own and likewise are starting to make their own decisions about what to read. Parents, teachers, librarians, and other "gatekeepers" still have a pronounced influence on the choices that middle graders make, so those adults will have to be comfortable with the subject matter. There's no room for sexual content of any kind in a middle grade book, and though action elements are a must, especially if you want boys to read your book, avoid graphic violence.

WRITING FOR CHILDREN

Fantasy for kids can still deal with significant issues, but you will have to tread carefully around, or avoid entirely, subjects like sex, politics, and religion. You have to take care in terms of reading level and vocabulary as well. There are a couple different methods to determine reading level. The SMOG Readability Formula (*http://niace.org.uk/development-research/readability*) and the Flesch-Kincaid Grade Level Index are both easy enough to apply. Microsoft Word will automatically determine the Flesch-Kincaid grade level as part of its grammar check function.

Though it would be nice to hope that a friendly acquisitions editor or agent will let you know if your book has stepped over the line in terms of content or reading level, then work with you to fix it, chances are you'll never get that chance. An editor or agent will probably move you from the "maybe" to the "no thanks" pile the second you cross one of those boundaries. Do your homework before you venture into the middle grade or younger worlds. Though it can seem like a minefield at times, there are maps out there. Lesley Bolton's *The Everything®️ Guide to Writing Children's Books* contains excellent advice for would-be children's authors in any genre.

To Sum Up

In her book *Are Women Human?* (Harvard University Press, 2006), Catherine A. MacKinnon wrote, "The pornographers know what pornography is." I think the same holds true with fantasy and science fiction. Fantasists and fantasy readers know what fantasy is. Likewise for science fiction authors and readers. Sometimes the distinction is overwhelmingly clear. Works like *The Hobbit, The Wonderful Wizard of Oz*, and *Beowulf* helped define the fantasy genre and provide strong benchmarks that we've all been building on since. The early works of Jules Verne and H. G. Wells drew the basic boundaries of science fiction. In some cases, the lines blur a bit, confusing editors, agents, booksellers, and even readers. But in the end, fantasy is fiction in which the impossible is possible without a logical explanation. Science fiction is where the impossible is possible with a logical explanation.

PART II
THE SIX STEPS

"Real seriousness in regard to writing is one of two absolute necessities. The other, unfortunately, is talent."

—ERNEST HEMINGWAY

Is it really as easy as following six simple steps—do this then that then the other, exactly in that order, six times in all—and in the end you've produced a perfect science fiction or fantasy novel? Of course not, and neither this section's heading, nor the book's subtitle, is meant to imply that. However, there are six major elements to a well-crafted science fiction or fantasy novel, elements that no author can afford to ignore or take lightly. You will find yourself bouncing back and forth between steps. Fear not. The creative process can feel messy at times, but only when it's working properly.

STEP ONE | STORYTELLING

"Fantasy's ability to serve as a perfect venue for moral questions is (among a few other things) what gives the genre its enduring strength."

—PAUL S. KEMP, the *New York Times* bestselling novelist and creator of Erevis Cale

Storytelling is at the heart of any genre of fiction. If you're a good natural storyteller, world building, research, sentence structure—the *craft* of writing—is something you can learn by heeding advice from books like this one, from helpful editors and English teachers, and so on. If you're not a good natural storyteller, you've got a long, difficult road ahead of you. Teaching writing is relatively easy, but teaching storytelling is close to impossible.

This section will cover the superstructure upon which all your world-building details and clever turns of phrase are supported. Idea, theme, plot . . . without them you can tell us all about the political structure of your fantasy world, create a whole new language and alphabet, portray a rich mythology or fantastical religion, but no one will ever know. You won't have finished a book, you'll have filled a notebook. You won't be done, you'll just be ready to start.

CHAPTER 4
START WITH AN IDEA

What is your book about?

Hollywood screenwriters use what they call a "log line" to describe a movie in twenty-five words or less. Crafting a clear log line for your novel is a good exercise to run through early on. It can help keep you focused as you write and help you describe your book to agents, editors, and readers when you're done.

A reluctant hero inherits a strange family heirloom that just happens to be at the center of the ultimate struggle of good against evil.

That's one way of describing The Lord of the Rings in twenty-four words.

A lost alien race has left behind working starships that intrepid prospectors take to unknown destinations across the galaxy in search of riches.

Frederick Pohl's *Gateway* in twenty-three words.

But where do ideas come from? Legendary author Harlan Ellison is famous for this profound answer:

> Go ahead, ask me the dumbest question a writer can be asked:
>
> "DUHH, WHERE D'YA GETCHER IDEAS?"
>
> My answer is always the same—since there is no answer to this query. At least neither Plato nor Socrates nor Shakespeare could make the codification. When some jamook asks me this one (thereby revealing him/herself to be a person who has about as much imaginative muscle as a head of lettuce), I always smile prettily and answer, "Schenectady."

And when the jamook looks at me quizzically, and scratches head with hairy hand, I add: "Oh, sure. There's a swell Idea Service in Schenectady; and every week I send 'em twenty-five bucks; and every week they send me a fresh six-pak of ideas."

And wouldja believe it . . . there is always some insufficient asshole who asks me for the address.

In fact that factory is not located in Schenectady, but in your head. Or if you prefer, in your soul, or your spirit—or ideas are handed to you from Jesus, or your muse, or the little mouse named Chitzy that lives in your limbic system.

Tolkien drew inspiration from myth and legend, as have countless authors before and since. Sometimes those myths and legends aren't ancient fables but contemporary tales of fantasy, like fantasy authors inspired by romance novels or the evolving vampire myth. A lot of the best science fiction and fantasy ideas start with the words "What if?"

What if a vampire became an agent for the CIA? What if a gnome from Iceland moved to a small town in Alaska and became a local hero? What if a suit of armor drives everyone who wears it insane? What if the best swordsman in the kingdom lost both his arms? What if the gods of Greek mythology were alive and well and working in the New York fashion business?

Where did these ideas come from? I have no idea. I just thought of them. And I mean literally, just this second as I typed this. Those ideas were not in my notes.

Sometimes ideas come from as mundane a source as the daily newspaper. Bestselling author of *The Sword of Shannara*, Terry Brooks often draws inspiration from current events: "Almost everything I write starts and ends with world and personal issues that countries and individuals struggle to resolve in the present."

THE TIMELESSNESS OF GOOD STORIES

R. A. Salvatore advises caution when relying on current events for inspiration, though he's known to do it himself. "One of my biggest problems," he admits, "is balancing the current events aspect with the story I'm trying to tell. Sometimes I get so angry over certain issues that I can't be satisfied unless I shout something, even if maybe, in the context of the fantasy book, I should have whispered."

One of the things a fantasy novel has going for it over science fiction, which is always in danger of seeming "dated," isn't its keen ear for contemporary issues, but its inherent timelessness. If the subject matter is too rooted in the here and now, fantasy and science fiction might not be interesting to readers in the elsewhere and later.

Don't just reinterpret that news item in the context of a fantasy story or imagine it forward to some point in the distant future. Instead, ask how that item speaks to a bigger, more timeless issue.

If, for instance, you're inspired by a story about the fight for or against same-sex marriage, is that what your novel is really about? Or is it about a minority group seeking acceptance and tolerance from the majority? Or about an amoral insurrection trying to destroy a religious and ethical lynchpin that could topple an entire culture? Now you have an idea that's both current and timeless, regardless of what side of the real-world argument you're on.

DRAWING FROM HISTORY

History is just current events that happened in the past. Novelist and video game writer Jess Lebow sometimes starts with a historical event and works from there. "History is a great place to start for basic conflicts. I figure if someone has started a war over an incident, then a reader will believe a character who takes offense at the same thing." Though he looks to history for inspiration, Lebow is just as likely to draw inspiration from his own experience. "I find myself jotting down little vignettes from daily life—things that seem absurd or amusing or just interesting in the way they played out. Sometimes I weave these together or into my work. Other times they just sit on the page, waiting for the right moment. I have every scrap of paper I've ever jotted on. None of the ideas are lost, but they certainly aren't organized."

You should maintain this kind of an idea file or notebook. If all you have is a napkin, write it on the napkin. Scrawl it in the steam on your shower door, or call your own voice mail and leave it there. Then try to forget about it. If you can't, it's probably a good idea.

Don't count out other authors as sources of inspiration. Though you'd be ill advised to copy your favorite fantasy or science fiction author, you can't help but be influenced, at least a little, by what you read. Terry Brooks has been. "Much of what I write, thematically," he said, "can be traced back to an early and enduring fascination with William Faulkner."

CHAPTER 5

HAVE SOMETHING TO SAY

What does your book teach us? You may not think you have anything to teach your readers. Maybe you just want to entertain them. You may think that if you keep the action flowing and present a likable hero and a despicable villain, that's plenty for a science fiction or fantasy novel, anyway. After all, maybe you're a fan (like me) of the "hack-and-slash" sword and sorcery stories of Robert E. Howard. The Conan stories didn't have anything to teach, did they? It was all about swinging battle-axes and rescuing damsels in distress, wasn't it?

In a famous letter to fellow *Weird Tales* contributor H. P. Lovecraft in the spring of 1932, Robert E. Howard wrote, "With the exception of one dream, I am never, in these dreams of ancient times, a civilized man. Always I am the barbarian, the skin-clad, tousle-haired, light-eyed wild man, armed with a rude axe or sword, fighting the elements and wild beasts, or grappling with armored hosts marching with the tread of civilized discipline, from fallow fruitful lands and walled cities. This is reflected in my writings, too, for when I begin a tale of old times, I always find myself instinctively arrayed on the side of the barbarian, against the powers of organized civilization."

This indicates that the Conan stories were *about* something. They had an intentional point of view. So, yes, fantasy and science fiction stories not only *can* have a message, but like all fiction, inherently *must* have a message. The subtlety with which that message is conveyed is another matter entirely.

THE MESSAGE IN THE NOVEL

Author Paul S. Kemp found inspiration in the Elric novels of Michael Moorcock, which expanded his conception of the fantasy genre and showed him, "that it could be more than warm, mostly light-hearted fare, and could, in fact, grapple with profound moral questions through the lens of a story well-told. Ultimately *that* is what made me want to write."

And it's what makes us want to read. Even if you didn't spend days after finishing The Lord of the Rings pondering the extent of the corrupting influence of power, had that idea not driven the book, I'll bet you wouldn't have liked it as much.

The theme of your novel is a choice only you can make. If you try to take a stand you don't believe in, your story will ring hollow. Your novel requires your unique political perspective, moral compass, ingrained ethics, religious beliefs, and worldview.

In an effort to focus those worldviews, we'll discuss five of the many universal themes that can get you thinking.

THE TRUE MEANING OF . . .

Evil? Power? Life? Civilization? What secrets do you have to share with your readers? Maybe you've thought about the true meaning of life and decided you might have something to add to the discussion. Tolstoy said that "the only absolute knowledge attainable by man is that life is meaningless." Did Tolstoy believe we have to find ways to give our own lives meaning—that the universe doesn't have a "meaning" mapped out for us at birth? If you agree, write a novel about it. If you disagree, write a novel about it. Most readers and editors are delighted to read stories with a message they don't necessarily agree with, and they are never happier than when they read something that changes their minds.

THE CORRUPTING INFLUENCE OF . . .

There's plenty to choose from here. Authors like J. R. R. Tolkien have been exploring the corrupting influence of power from the Oedipus plays of Sophocles through Peter Morgan's *Frost/Nixon* and beyond. And what about money? In fantasy, money can take the form of anything from gold pieces to magic-infused crystals. Frank Herbert's classic science fiction novel *Dune* was about the corrupting influence of money in the form of natural resources—and it's clear he was really talking about oil—which he reimagined as the spice melange.

THE VITAL IMPORTANCE OF . . .

Not everything has to be corrupting. The movie *The Fifth Element* was all about the vital importance of love. Robert E. Howard wrote about the vital importance of the individual in his first short story, "Spear and Fang," published in *Weird Tales* in 1925. *The Fountainhead* by Ayn Rand, which covers much of the same philosophical territory, came eighteen years later in 1943.

Ask yourself a simple question that could be very difficult to answer: What do you think is most vital in life? Then think of a fantasy or science fiction story that explores that theme. Home and family? *The Wonderful Wizard of Oz.* Faith? *Left Behind.* Friendship and acceptance? *The Crystal Shard.*

THE UNDENIABLE POWER OF . . .

Some things we can't avoid, stop, or manipulate. Science fiction authors were among the first to imagine the worst outcomes of global climate change. And natural forces aren't the only things that we can all agree are "undeniable." Spider-Man is about the undeniable power of personal responsibility. Whether or not Peter Parker chooses to take responsibility for his powers, it's clear that "with great power comes great responsibility."

THE ETERNAL STRUGGLE BETWEEN . . .

Good and evil is the easiest counter position, almost too easy. If you dress a character up in a Nazi SS uniform, he's the bad guy. No offense to Indiana Jones, but think deeper than that. At what point do good and evil meet? Can someone working for the clear cause of good go too far? Is evil an expression of good that you don't agree with? Man versus nature appears here too, and in fantasy and science fiction you can imagine a world in which man has won that fight, or thinks he has—was that a good thing?

This just begins to scratch the surface, but I hope it will get you thinking in terms of what it is you want to say. Fiction doesn't communicate pithy dialog and nail-biting action, it communicates *ideas,* through pithy dialog and nail-biting action.

CHAPTER 6
DEVELOP A PLOT

Plot is born out of conflict. But what does that mean? In most science fiction or fantasy novels, it's exactly what it sounds like: a conflict (often physical) between the hero and the villain, representing the battle between good and evil. But you don't have to limit your thinking in that way. The terms *protagonist* and *antagonist*, which are fancy ways of saying *hero* and *villain*, are useful if you have a tendency to—or are purposely trying to avoid—judging your characters.

Though no plot is entirely limited to one hero and one villain, they are the principal drivers. And of course the hero and the villain can both be men, women, or one of each. The princess can be a prince. Both of them can be dragons. There is no rule—anymore, at least—that a hero has to be a white man. Sometimes two heroes or two villains are in conflict with each other. Sometimes the character you think is the hero at the beginning of story turns out to be the villain in the end. Then there are stories in which the villain isn't a thinking being at all, but the immutable forces of nature, the hero's own prejudices or preconceptions, and so on.

This means your novel doesn't need to fall back on a steely eyed Lancelot versus a fascistic Dr. Doom. But unless your protagonist comes into conflict—in the broadest sense of the word—with someone or something, you have no plot, no story, and no novel.

STORY IS ESSENTIAL

"The story remains essential to human beings," says Ethan Ellenberg, a literary agent who heads the eponymous Ethan Ellenberg Literary Agency. "It's a better organizer of life than philosophy or ethics or nearly any other human endeavor I can think of."

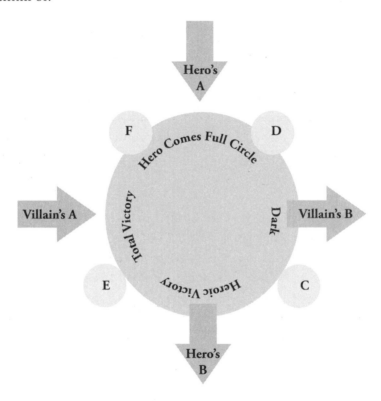

In the figure above, the arrow that points down to the top of the circle is the beginning of the hero's A-B line. The hero starts somewhere—a quiet little medieval village or at the helm of a starship—but has a burning need or desire to do something, like find the indigo lotus that will end the terrible scalp-pox epidemic that threatens to destroy the kingdom, or complete the Kessel Run in less than twelve parsecs.

At the same time (or around the same time), the villain starts from the other A—maybe a dungeon cell or the control room of a space station—also with a burning desire, such as to find the indigo lotus so he can decide who is cured of the scalp-pox, or to enslave the indigenous sentient primitives of the planet Rigel-238.

Often the hero and the villain are after the same or similar goals, but for different reasons and with different intended results. However, it can be even more interesting if they start out with entirely different objectives. For instance, what if the hero begins with the goal of paying off the family farm and living happily ever after with the girl of his dreams? The villain, on the other hand, wants to kill half the people in the realm with the scalp-pox, a disease he created in an alchemical laboratory in order to receive thanks, recognition, and other great favors by eventually saving the realm with the magic healing powers of the indigo lotus.

HERO AND VILLAIN INTERSECT

When we get to the center circle, the plot of our novel takes shape. This is the territory in which the hero's A-B line meets the villain's A-B line, and the story begins in earnest. Carrying forward the previous example, the hero's girlfriend falls victim to the scalp-pox, so the hero sets off to find a cure and (maybe literally) bumps into the villain, who's also looking for the indigo lotus. The plot then hinges on a race to find the healing flower.

Like two hockey pucks bumping into each other on the ice, when those two lines meet, they send each other off into different trajectories, ending at C, D, E, or F. In the diagram, those new trajectories end up between the A-B lines, but how your plot plays out and ends is based on the angle of deflection.

The space between C and D is labeled "Dark," between C and E is "Heroic Victory", between E and F is "Total Victory," and between F and D is "Hero Comes Full Circle."

Hero Comes Full Circle

Means the story ends closer to the hero's beginning point. We'll see the hero back home, but not necessarily living happily ever after. He has achieved a qualified victory over the villain. The closer this moves to point D, the darker that gets. Maybe the hero has found the lotus only to realize it's too late to save his girlfriend, but the kingdom will benefit. Move it closer to F and she lives.

Total Victory

Ends not only with the hero defeating the villain but deflecting the villain back to near the villain's own point A. If the villain was trying to become the absolute ruler of the realm, in this ending, he's back in the dungeon cell.

Heroic Victory

Means the hero has not only defeated the villain but has come to the end of his own A-B line. He's progressed as a person more than he might in a "Total Victory" ending. Likely he's had to sacrifice something along the way. He's been deflected from his goals by the villain's actions, but he wins the day in the end. In this example maybe he's cured everyone of the scalp-pox but himself.

Dark

Is the province of the "downer ending" in which the villain actually wins the day. In this ending, maybe the hero has managed to save his girlfriend from the scalp-pox, but the villain still becomes king. The hero has won only a partial victory at best and we end with the villain laughing with maniacal satisfaction.

Play with that diagram and think about how a story can change depending on how those A-B lines bounce around inside the circle.

Author Jess Lebow offers these words of advice: "Remember Newton's Third Law of Motion—for every action there is an equal and opposite reaction. In other words, for every move your protagonist takes, the antagonist driving the conflict in the scene (be that a character, an environment, or a circumstance) needs to make one too. The only time this stops is when the conflict is fully resolved."

CHAPTER 7

KNOW WHEN TO STOP

Fantasy novels seem to come in trilogies, and even science fiction, a little less sequel-oriented than its magical cousin, can explode out into multi-book series. There is no clear rule of thumb as to why and when you should start thinking beyond one book. However, agent Ethan Ellenberg advises caution: "The first book must be a completely satisfying stand-alone novel. Too often I'll read a first in a trilogy book that will be 'saving' a lot of the plot for the future books, and it mars the first book."

Let's start with how big your story needs to be. Jess Lebow begins by thinking in terms of length at the outline stage: "It's important to know where you are going before you begin. Even if you don't end up writing the whole trilogy, it really helps develop the world if you know what happened before and after the book you're writing."

"I've done it both ways, actually," admits R. A. Salvatore. "The irony is that in my longest-running series, the Drizzt books, I only plan them out one at a time. I think of Sherlock Holmes or James Bond as my guides here, where even though it's a long series, The Legend of Drizzt is really a series of adventures following a cast of characters walking down a winding and interesting road. By contrast, when I did the original DemonWars Saga, I knew where the seven books were going to take me. DemonWars is really one story, and I wouldn't recommend reading the fourth or the fifth without reading the ones that came before. With Drizzt, pick it up anywhere; hopefully you'll have enough fun to go back and learn what came before, but I try to make sure that knowledge isn't essential to enjoying the latest adventure."

HOW BIG A BOOK?

Laura Resnick's *The White Dragon* is a terrific, richly realized fantasy, the first part of *In Fire Forged*, which is the sequel to the stand-alone novel *In Legend Born*. But it sure feels like the second book in a trilogy (which ends with *The Destroyer Goddess*). In an Author's Note at the end of *The White Dragon*, Laura tells us that *In Fire Forged* was written as one book but ended up being so long that they decided to publish it as two books. A book can only be so thick.

These are the things publishers suffer over, but very few readers even notice. Readers enjoy books if they like the story, the characters, the writing . . . the important stuff. Numbering books in a series can help people read them in the right order, but lately the book trade has been frowning on this practice, since it can be hard to keep every book in a series on the shelf of every store in a nationwide chain. If all you see on the shelf is Book II, you might just move on to another series rather than ask to special order Book I. But if that fact is less apparent, and the second book is sufficiently self-contained, you might be inclined to jump into the series at that point, and the sale is made.

Hugo-nominated editorial director of Pyr books and the editor of several critically acclaimed anthologies, Lou Anders, told me, "There is nothing better than a series that works and that builds from book to book. And there is nothing worse than taking something on and knowing that each successive book is going to do less well than the one before it." Anders uses the word "risky" when it comes to first-time authors planning on more than a "stand-alone novel with the potential of a follow-up." However, he admits to occasionally betting on a series from a new author.

Still, allow a prospective publisher to take a cautious approach. Most editors aren't entirely the Lords and Ladies of the Manor they'd like to be. Most if not all are answerable to editorial boards and business managers who need to be reassured that the publishing house's money is being well and carefully spent. A presentation to an editorial board that starts off "I have a great new eighteen-book mega-series by this awesome up-and-coming young author" can be scary for everyone involved. "I have a great fantasy book by a fantastic new author that people are going to love" is liable to get a better reception, even if you and your editor have a good feeling that if all goes well you've got seventeen more books in the hopper.

Author Paul S. Kemp follows a simple rule: "I always weave threads into my current novel with an eye toward expanding them in a later book, should the opportunity arise. These are tangential notes/characters—just little plot seeds—about which/whom I've got ideas for expanding the story."

Regardless of whether or not your story demands a sequel, Lou Anders further cautions against resting too long before starting on the next project. "You really risk your career when you take more than a year between books now, at least before you are established, and in this media-centric world of near-infinity choice, where many publishers (Pyr included) are experimenting with publishing books in a series in consecutive months, waiting more than a year for book two is going to cost you eyeballs. Because plenty of shiny objects are going to intrude between now and then. Finish the book, type 'The end,' and then open a new file and start the next one right away!"

And be ready to change direction on a dime if your editor asks for something new.

CHAPTER 8
LEARN HOW TO WRITE

I promised I wouldn't spend too much time on the nuts and bolts of writing—grammar, punctuation, usage, that kind of stuff—but would keep my eye on the real purpose of this book, advice for the aspiring science fiction and fantasy author. Watch my blog (*http:// fantasyhandbook.wordpress.com*) for more dos and don'ts on the craft of writing. Like just about everyone who's ever taken seriously the idea of writing for a living, you'll have to wade through multiple sources for the best advice on the craft. But the stakes are high. According to author John Betancourt, "Aspiring authors not only have to write well, but they have to write better than their competitors—in this case, authors who are currently publishing. So the bar is raised with every generation."

Even then, as bestselling author Paul S. Kemp says, "No one masters writing. It cannot be done. But if you thoughtfully analyze your own work, read widely (especially outside of genre), take what you can of value from accomplished authors, you'll improve. And that's all you can ever do."

There might be thousands of books on the craft of writing, and many of them are good. I'll recommend a few specifically on my blog from time to time, but look on your own. Flip through books, scan tables of contents, and consider feedback you've received from others. For instance, if you've been told that your writing is "passive," or you have a tendency to use comma splices, look up those terms in particular and learn what you're doing, study how to do it differently, and experiment with ways to improve your writing.

SOME LITERARY TERMS

As you look through advice on writing, you're probably going to come across the following terms.

Voice

Every author, every novel, should sound unique. What makes your novel different from mine, and mine different from Terry Brooks's, and Terry's different from Lord Dunsany's—and so on—is an ethereal concept we call "voice." This is the turn of phrase, the rhythm of writing, the presentation of ideas that makes your writing entirely your own. No one can teach that. You can't even teach it to yourself. It just happens, and the more you try to force it the more obviously forced, the less natural, it will become, and your writing will suffer.

Place

Without a well-considered sense of place your characters are wandering through a gray void, talking to each other like characters in a cheap one-act off-Broadway play. No offense to cheap one-act off-Broadway plays—they have a brilliance all their own—but you're writing a novel (or a short story) and so have an unlimited "budget" for set design or location shooting. Your story can take place *anywhere*. Fantasy should take place in fantastic surroundings and science fiction should be set in a richly realized future—surroundings that become characters in themselves.

J. M. McDermott, critically acclaimed author of the novel *Last Dragon*, feels that "a sense of place is more than just where a table is standing, or whether the walls are blue or orange. Sense of place is really about a sense of meaning felt about the place. That can come from the physical reality of the space. Even better is when the sense of place comes from the meaning that the space has for the characters."

None of this means you should spend tortuous page after page dutifully recording the measurements of every room, listing the materials used in its construction, reporting the temperature in both Fahrenheit and Centigrade, and so on. It means that your characters have to have a place to live in that's at least as alive as they are.

"A sense of place is much harder to convey if there is no touchstone from our own world," says Terry Brooks. "If the place is imaginary, the writer has to work much harder to permit the reader to connect. Use all five senses to draw the reader in. Find something unusual for the important places, something the reader will easily remember. Use place to set mood. Remember that place in a fantasy story is always a character."

As you write, include as many of the five senses as possible:

Sight. If your characters walk into a room, what does the room look like? This could include all sorts of detail: "The walls were the color of summer leaves" (a fancy way of saying *green*) "and the floor was tiled in exquisitely veined marble mined from the Frostbite Crags by Hillgrumble miners of the Floorington Clan . . . ." Ask yourself: What is this room and why is the scene taking place there? Maybe it's the emperor's throne room. Is the emperor an ostentatious man? If so, the room is probably really big and richly decorated. Is the emperor a no-nonsense former general, so the room is Spartan and austere? Maybe both: "The emperor, a no-nonsense former general, seemed out of place in the richly decorated, cavernous throne room built by his ostentatious predecessor."

Think about what the place is used for and what significance it has to the scene as well as the characters. Know who lives or works there, and design accordingly. Remember, it can look however you want it to look, from a simple drawing room sparsely furnished in Amish hardwoods to a room bigger than any room in the real world, in which millions of people have gathered to hang on the emperor's every word.

Smell. What would a room filled with millions of people smell like? "Despite the seemingly endless throngs of petitioners, drawn from all corners of the empire, the room smelled of jingle flowers, the empress's favorite, perfectly balanced, never overpowering, just enough to remind every living soul there of the presence of their queen." So now the smell tells us something about the people who exist in that place, and not just that they're all sweaty.

Feel. Rooms aren't necessarily rough or smooth, but they can be cold or hot, right? And maybe the walls *are* rough. Why would that matter? "When the emperor pushed the disobedient courtier against the wall, the razorlike stucco cut into the back of his head deeply enough that he felt hot blood trickle down the back of his neck." This tells us that the emperor is not to be messed with, and the room carries that vibe as well.

Sound. "The roar of millions of voices was deafening, but when the trumpets blared to announce the prince's arrival, a hush descended over the gathering as though a heavy curtain had been drawn around those assembled." Places don't necessarily have a sound, but the people and things inside them do. How does sound echo in that space? If the scene is taking place outside, are there crickets? Something like crickets but an animal or strange chirping plant of your own creation? What does that sound tell the reader about the place? Those trumpets interrupting millions of conversations could mean that the people are afraid of the prince. Or does it mean they love the prince and can't wait to hear what he has to say?

Taste. This one is hard. Rooms don't usually have a taste, but could the air have one? Is there a smell so thick—either pleasant or unpleasant—that the characters can actually taste it? Is the room full of water—saltwater or stagnant, or perfumed? You may have to skip this one, and let four of the five senses convey a sense of place, but don't pass without thinking about it first!

Point of View

Some authors tell me they write in "third person omniscient," which they take to mean that the unseen, unnamed narrator somehow knows something the characters don't. To my mind there is no difference between "third person omniscient" and "third person lazy." In any one scene, choose one character and get into his or her (or its!) head and stay there until you decide you need to switch to someone else's head. If it makes sense to end the chapter there, do so. Otherwise, a scene break is fine. But limit those point-of-view (POV) shifts so you aren't stopping your readers every few paragraphs.

"I don't like shifting POV unless there is a clear break in scene and setting and even time," Terry Brooks told me. "I like chapters to mostly stick with one character and one POV. It isn't that you can't manage to juggle multiple POVs. It's more that sticking with one lends the chapter consistency and cohesion. Too much jumping around tends to break down the reader's connection with the characters."

PRACTICE MAKES BETTER

In a famous joke, a guy asks a bellhop in New York City how to get to Carnegie Hall. The bellhop answers, "Practice, practice, practice." Write a lot, keep thinking about what you're doing, take it seriously, and you'll get better.

But even with all that practice there's as much to the art and craft of writing that can't be learned as there is that can. "Great writing has a certain magical energy that elevates it above the mundane," says literary agent Ethan Ellenberg. "It's very hard to be good if you don't have that."

Practice can make you a better writer, but in the final analysis it comes down to talent, a gift, whatever you call it. In the immortal words of *Gypsy*'s Mama Rose, "Either you got it, or you ain't."

To Sum Up

Storytelling is hard, but it means everything. You can learn some basics, but mostly it comes from within, refined with practice.

Though a log line—the twenty-five word description of your novel—can feel contrived, it can be useful in keeping your eye on the heart of your story. Consider starting the log line with the words "What if?"

Look for inspiration in myth and legend, current events, history, your own life, or the work of other authors, but look behind the news clipping for the fundamental conflict or question beneath it. Even the most broadly realized sword and sorcery adventure novel should have something to say. Some of your hardest work will come from balancing truth and fiction, style and substance. Start thinking about those five universal truths, and come up with at least five more of your own.

Plot is all about the point at which the villain's plans and the hero's plans collide, and both find new trajectories. The geometry, like the nature and identities of the hero and villain, is entirely up to you.

Choose the length of your story with care. In the current publishing climate, I recommend a stand-alone novel with series potential over anything written to be part of a trilogy or longer series—but do yourself a favor and sprinkle in plot hooks for future stories. You never know.

Study the craft of writing, and keep writing until you find your voice. To establish a sense of place, think carefully about the "whys" of the place: Why is it there? Why is it the setting for this scene? Then tell us only what we need to know to give the action context, appealing to as many of the five senses as possible.

And one scene, one POV, every single time.

STEP TWO | CHARACTERS

"All great stories, whatever the genre,
begin with great characters."

—LOU ANDERS

Fiction has always been, continues to be, and always will be about someone doing something. In the last section we talked about ideas and plots, which is essentially what the character is doing. I put it in that order, but you don't have to. You can—maybe even should—start with an idea for a character *then* think about what you want him or her (or it!) to do, and why.

In this section I'll continue to use the words *hero* and *villain*, but with the same caveat as before: the villain doesn't have to be what video game writer Jess Lebow calls "a mustache-twirling, cape-wearing hooligan who runs around trying to tie women to the train tracks." The villain could be a blizzard, a meteor, or someone who thinks he's a hero. And the hero can be someone who'd rather not go on an adventure at all, like Bilbo Baggins in *The Hobbit.* The hero can even start out as the villain, like Vin Diesel as Riddick in the movie *Pitch Black.* And, of course, both hero and villain can be either gender, and like Bilbo, doesn't even have to be human. Likewise, play with what it means to be a hero or a villain, and challenge your readers to think about how your characters fit into those categories.

J. M. McDermott hopes "to get to a point, in fantasy fiction, where there is neither a hero nor a villain. I hope we get to the point where there are just people, doing the best they can with what they have, and building or destroying the world around them and the people around them as part of the things that make those characters who they are."

CHAPTER 9

ASK, AND ANSWER, QUESTIONS

What makes a character "compelling"? Start by making him (or her, or it—assume for the rest of the book that I don't believe any sort of character has to be either gender, or human, even if all I say is "he" or "him") as fully realized a person as you can muster. Don't just start writing, spend some time thinking. Jot down notes, but don't be afraid to scratch them out and replace them with better ideas. Not all of your notes will make it into the book, but the more you know about your characters—villain and hero alike—the more life those characters will have on the page.

Don't even name your characters yet. We'll talk later about language and naming conventions, which you should consider before you settle on names, so for now in your notes, use placeholders like HERO, VILLAIN, LOVE INTEREST, FOIL, WISE MAN, and so on.

Author J. M. McDermott finds inspiration for characters from people he knows in real life. "To me, art is a celebration of being human among humans, and a way to make sense of the whole, messy affair. I often quietly steal my friends and close relations for stories—though you'd likely never know if I didn't tell you. For instance 'Fest Fasen' [a character in his critically acclaimed first novel *Last Dragon*] was loosely based on my friend Ben Fasenfest. Ben was definitely not anything like the character Fest Fasen in age or action or goals, but Ben was a way to start thinking about the character. Starting with that core of someone I felt like I knew gave me the Claymation skeleton upon which I could pile exceptionally thick layers of clay."

Here are the six questions anyone should start with when first thinking about a character. These questions aren't unlike the basic approach that journalists take when they sit down to write a story.

1. Who is the character? Consider the possibilities. *He's the second son of a noble family who's forced into the priesthood of a faith he doesn't believe in.* Or *She's an alien disguised as a human woman who fears she may be the last of her species to survive the Black Hole Wars.*

2. Where did he come from? Keeping with the previous examples: *He's the second son of a noble family from the fringes of the empire who's forced into the priesthood of a faith he doesn't believe in, because his creepy uncle is a high priest.* So now we know this is a small-town boy with family connections he's not happy about. *She's an alien disguised as a human woman, a stranger from a distant planet, wandering lost in a human moon settlement, who fears she may be the last of her species to survive the Black Hole Wars.*

The answer to this question doesn't have to be geographical. Where does he come from—spiritually? Maybe he comes from a fringe political group.

3. What is he doing? This is the A of his A-B line before he intersects with the villain (if he's a hero) or with the hero (if he's a villain). *He's the second son of a noble family from the fringes of the empire who's forced into the priesthood of a faith he doesn't believe in, because his creepy uncle is a high priest. He plans to escape the church, but may have to bring down both his uncle and his father to do it.* Now he has a plan, which already conflicts with someone else's plans.

She's an alien disguised as a human woman, a stranger from a distant planet, wandering lost in a human moon settlement, who fears she may be the last of her species to survive the Black Hole Wars. But the computer implanted in her brain provides the genetic coding to repopulate her homeworld. She's come to the moon to find a rare element that will guarantee the success of the mass cloning, an element the moon colony was built to protect. That sounds like a difficult mission, which is good. Easily accomplished missions rarely make for interesting stories.

4. Why is he doing it? "Why not?" or "If he doesn't, there's no story" are never good enough answers. If that's all you can come up with, then for goodness sake, don't start writing. One of the clearest signs of an inexperienced author is a weak eye toward character motivation. *Why* a character does *anything* is critical. Spend days on this one alone. Try to debunk a character's motivations. Keep thinking, keep asking questions, until you can't think of anything else to ask. And that's not when you're done, it's when you start.

As you're writing, you'll find yourself constantly circling back to that *why* question. Never shrug that off. If it drags your writing to a complete stop, good. Stop. Think. Support your characters and get started again, even if it means a radical left turn in what you thought your story was going to be. There is no story compelling enough to support unmotivated characters.

He's the second son of a noble family from the fringes of the empire who's forced into the priesthood of a faith he doesn't believe in, because his creepy uncle is a high priest. He plans to escape the church, and may have to bring down both his uncle and his father to do it, because he really wanted to stay home and marry a pretty farm girl he's been in love with his whole life. Sounds like a plan that could be tragically interrupted, but one we can sympathize with.

Suppose our alien woman swore to her father on his deathbed that she would save their species, a grand culture spanning hundreds of star systems with a million years of cultural and technological achievements the galaxy would suffer greatly to lose. Well, we'd all like to think of ourselves as heroic enough to fight against all odds for the survival of our species, and that's certainly a worthy goal for any science fiction character. But providing some kind of personal hook will make your character come alive not just as the last of a once-great culture but as a person. That deathbed promise to her father, or a heartfelt profession of undying love from our reluctant priest, tells us why she or he is *personally* involved in the story, even while serving a greater good.

5–6. How will he do it? and **What's at stake?** are two questions that drive the entire plot of your story. But what he thinks is going to happen, or what he wants to happen, will change as he starts to bump into other characters and situations. There's an old saying in the military that "no plan survives contact with the enemy." That's the root of storytelling. But if you don't start with a "plan," it'll be hard for your readers to know when it's gone off the rails. And if you haven't clearly defined what's at stake, your readers will never know why the fact that it's gone off the rails is so bad.

He's the second son of a noble family from the fringes of the empire who's forced into the priesthood of a faith he doesn't believe in, because his creepy uncle is a high priest. He plans to escape the church because he really wanted to stay home and marry a pretty farm girl he's been in love with his whole life. But the only way he can think of to escape the church is to aid the invading forces of a rival faith, who will grant him his freedom when the fortress-like temple is sacked. But the rivals insist on burning his uncle at the stake, and his father is only in the position he's in because of the support of the temple, so when the temple falls, his father will lose his clanhold. Can he use the rival faith to help him escape the temple without wiping it off the map and destroying his generally well-meaning father? Can he "have his cake and eat it too?"

Here we have the hero's plan—escape from the temple and marry his sweetheart—bumping into the villain's plan: wipe out the temple. Now we have a hero who wants to achieve his own goals but isn't willing to do that at all cost. He's in a tough spot, and tough spots make compelling stories.

She's an alien disguised as a human woman, a stranger from a distant planet, wandering lost in a human moon settlement, who fears she may be the last of her species to survive the Black Hole Wars. But the computer implanted in her brain provides the genetic coding to repopulate her homeworld. She's come to the moon to find a rare element that will guarantee the success of the mass cloning, an element the moon colony was built to protect. In order to save her species and make good on a promise she made to her dying father, she worms her way into the colony's security forces, and eventually sneaks down into the lunar vaults to retrieve the rare element. She then realizes that the process of mass cloning requires the organic molecules in the human colonists' own bodies. It'll work, but it will kill everyone in the colony in the process. Is she really ready to do that? Especially since she started to feel something for the colony administrator—could it be love?

Here too the goals of the heroine will inflict unnecessary pain on innocents should she succeed, but I've added a second, unplanned complication: she meant to use the colony administrator but has found herself falling in love with him. And in this example we haven't even met a villain yet.

MORE QUESTIONS

In reality, creating characters is a long and involved process in which you will gather information by starting with these simple questions and asking many more. Likely you'll end up with pages and pages of notes on each of your main characters. Here are some additional questions I have about the alien disguised as a woman:

- Is she really prepared to sacrifice ten thousand human lives to save her dead race?
- Was it even a bad thing that they went extinct in the first place?
- Were they leaders of goodly nature, or monsters who ravaged the galaxy?
- How long has it been since she's spoken with another of her kind?
- Did the Black Hole Wars take place a year ago, or a thousand years ago?
- Should she simply ask the colonists for help?
- Would they help her, or be horrified by the revelation that she's actually an alien and immediately betray her to the xenophobic security forces?

Every question you ask about a character begets at least one more. Ask those questions, answer them in as many ways as you can think of, toss out the answers you don't like, and start asking follow-up questions to the answers you do like. Keep doing that, over and over and over again, until you've found your cast of characters.

And when do you know you have that cast in place? You may always have more questions to ask, but when you can't think of any more, start writing.

But which character do you start asking questions about first?

CHAPTER 10

START WITH THE VILLAIN

"There's a moment in James Enge's wonderful *Blood of Ambrose*," editor Lou Anders recalls, "where the villain, Lord Urdhven, the Protector, who has murdered his sister and brother-in-law for power, is actually quite heroic, and the novel takes time to reflect that in actuality, probably a great many perfectly good rulers came into power in less than honorable ways."

In Chapter 6, I offered a diagram that showed the villain's A-B line, and we discussed how a story begins to take on some life once that line intersects with the hero's A-B line. It's not at all uncommon, especially in traditional fantasy, for the villain to drive the plot forward. Heroes, time and again, begin as simple folk, or young people wanting little from life but love, stability, and the pursuit of happiness. That certainly describes Tolkien's Bilbo Baggins, Frank Herbert's Paul Atreides . . . any number of reluctant heroes. But the villain almost never has that luxury.

Mysteries usually begin with a murder, and the detective (hero) comes in only after the heinous act has been committed—*by the villain.* Fantasy and science fiction are hardly different, though the circumstances of what Hollywood formula-mongers would call the "inciting incident" are a touch more imaginative. Having a compelling, intimidating (or unpredictable, or scary, or . . . ?), three-dimensional villain is vital to the success of your story.

Though he's more than a little reluctant to enter into the distinction between hero and villain, novelist J. M McDermott describes villains as people "who abuse others for their own self-interest. It's a

symbol of their fundamental disconnection from the love that drives
human society."

IT'S ALL ABOUT MOTIVATION

If the villain plans to murder the Chosen of Jubilé because there
is no clear successor and the Church of the Revealed Truth will
descend into anarchy, allowing his own Cult of the Blue Oyster to
move in and fill the role of First Religion of the Empire, we need
to know why, so *ask questions*. Is he an evil genius, bent on world
domination? (Please, tell me you're not going to try to rest on that
old chestnut.) Is he still bitter about having been cast out of the
Church of the Revealed Truth when he discovered that the eighth of
the Fourteen Revelations was stolen from the Twentyfold Writings
of Frogam, a heretical religion the Church of the Revered Truth once
led a crusade against? Now you're talking. His methods (murder)
may make him a villain, but his history (the revelation of religious
hypocrisy) makes him a murderer we can understand.

"Giving a villain at least one redeeming quality can add a lot of
depth to the story," advises author Jess Lebow. "If the reader can
relate to him, even on a small level, then you have more tools with
which to create an emotional experience."

On that same note, Paul S. Kemp endeavors "to set up a situation
where the villain has a desire, a reasonable one, that puts him/her in
conflict with the hero."

So think about where the villain came from and why he's doing
what he's doing, but think carefully. A villain can be weakened
beyond repair if you spend too much of your creative energy trying
to make his motivations sympathetic. Continuing our example, if
it turns out that the Church of the Revealed Truth is really a cor-
rupt cabal of politicians-in-clerical-garb, their religion based on a
lie, then the villain's efforts to tear them down actually makes him a
hero—assuming his Cult of the Blue Oyster isn't even worse.

Again, look to historical figures, myth and legend, current events, or your own life for inspiration. Adolph Hitler was without doubt a villain, and one whose actions (coming to power through intimidation and assassination in the first place, invading Poland, establishing the death camps) intersected with the A-B line of the rest of the world and resulted in World War II. But at some point he was just baby Adolph—an infant, a clean slate. This is where we start asking questions: What happened that made him murderously anti-Semitic? What gave him the arrogance to think that his every whim could suffice as the law of the land? It's possible to make Adolph Hitler into a plausible villain when you take into account his experiences as a soldier on the losing side of World War I, his life as a failed artist during the crippling depression that followed, and the endemic anti-Semitism of 1920s Germany, but none of that excuses the period of grotesque genocide, stifling fascism, and brutal imperialism that he eventually engineered. At some point, Adolph Hitler chose to do the wrong thing. *He made himself a villain.*

Let's get back to the example of the Church of the Revealed Truth. Maybe no one now in the service of the church had anything to do with this plagiarism, which was perpetrated centuries ago, and the church is in fact the greatest stabilizing influence our otherwise chaotic fantasy world has ever experienced. The Chosen of Jubilé is an utterly altruistic heroine, a tireless champion of the common people, and if one little story in the ages-old scripture of her faith turns out to agree with a fraction of the heretical writings of a mad prophet, it won't erase the positive influence the rest has had on the world. At the same time, the villain's cult represents the darkest component of the human psyche, and fueled by the villain's overwhelming bitterness, it has resurrected human sacrifice and demon worship. Now we get why he's doing it, but we'd rather he didn't.

And that's the definition of a well-crafted villain: someone whose motivations we understand but whose methods we find abhorrent.

CHAPTER 11

NURTURE YOUR HEROES

If a villain is someone whose motivations we understand but whose methods we find abhorrent, a hero is someone whose motivations we understand and whose methods we find inspirational. Heroes come in all shapes and sizes, from Dorothy, the timid, reluctant protagonist from *The Wonderful Wizard of Oz* to the hyper-capable, resolute, and incorruptible Superman. It might be a tough row to hoe, creating Superman in the twenty-first century. Audiences are more sophisticated now—or are they?

What's so sophisticated about Harry Potter? He's a nice kid trying to find his way in a strange new environment, but he's far from edgy. One of the fantasy genre's most popular characters is R. A. Salvatore's dark elf Drizzt Do'Urden. Drizzt has a dark side and a tragic back-story that Harry Potter might lack, but still he's a good man—well, elf—trying to do the right thing in a chaotic world that doesn't always accept him for who he is.

You might find yourself pressured—by yourself if not from some other source—to reject the "hero" in full. All sorts of people, from bloggers to fellow fantasy fans, will tell you that the era of "simplistic" or "unsophisticated" heroic fantasy is over, and that the anti-hero, the dark, brooding, shadowy "Dark Knight" archetype is not only the big new trend but the only acceptable approach for fantasy or science fiction in the twenty-first century.

Okay, but then the 2008 Drizzt novel, *The Pirate King*, debuted at number three on the *New York Times* hardcover fiction bestsellers list, and Harry Potter made J. K. Rowling the most successful novelist of all time—rocketing past Stephen King like nothing the publishing industry has ever seen.

The hero is dead, long live the hero.

A COMPELLING PROTAGONIST

I fully support the hero, but I'm not advising that you create two-dimensional anythings, much less heroes. What we have to ask ourselves is: What makes a *compelling* hero?

Author Mike Resnick, who was named by *Locus* magazine as the all-time leading award winner, living or dead, for short fiction, doesn't think there's any one thing that defines a character as a hero. However, Resnick notes, "There is one thing that makes him a *boring* hero: no flaws. You start by making him as real (as opposed to heroic) within the context of the plot and setting, as you can. And you try to remember that if your Protagonist, a word I much prefer to Hero, doesn't have doubts and fears and misgivings to overcome, it's a lot less heroic to face an enemy of any type or proportion."

Indeed, but the advice from the previous section to avoid weakening villains applies here, too. Heroes must have flaws, but they must not be overwhelmed by them. They have to overcome those flaws as the story progresses. It's a popular adage that courage is the ability to work through your fears, not to be fearless, and a hero should be courageous in that manner. If Bilbo Baggins wasn't afraid of the dragon Smaug, how boring would *The Hobbit* have been? Another enduring hero, Spider-Man, is riddled with insecurities, deals with the tragic death of his uncle, and mourns the parents who died before we ever met him. He has financial woes, girlfriend troubles, and a nasty boss, but he still manages to do the right thing.

"Everyone comes from somewhere," editor Lou Anders cautions. "Everyone is defined by their relationships, their background, their history, their idiosyncrasies, their compromises, their wounds, their victories. Everyone married knows that you don't just marry your spouse, you marry their family as well, and in the same way, the lone hero who comes from nowhere, has no past, has no associations, has no quirks beyond being 'heroic' is as flat as a pancake."

Spider-Man comes from a working-class neighborhood in Queens and carries that background with him on his adventures. Similarly, Drizzt Do'Urden has a troubled past that colors his relationship with everyone he meets. His mother tried to sacrifice him to the Spider Queen, and his sisters were, well, let's say, "less than nurturing." Where do these back-stories come from? They come from the authors' decision to ask and answer the same series of questions you asked and answered to create your villain.

J. M. McDermott gave this definition of a hero: "Heroic figures, in heroic fiction, tend to put the good of others before their own good, as a symbol of the fundamental connection to the love that drives human society."

Let your hero be the person you wish you could be, and chances are, he'll be the person your readers wish they could be, too.

CHAPTER 12

GATHER YOUR SUPPORTING CHARACTERS

The classic science fiction short story "Life Hutch" by Harlan Ellison (his second published story) tells the tale of an astronaut named Terrence who takes cover in an automated shelter where he encounters a malfunctioning robot that will kill him if he moves a muscle. This is the only story I can think of that has no supporting characters, though even then some hostile aliens, the Kyben, are mentioned as the reason Terrence has found himself in this sticky predicament in the first place.

An author as talented as Harlan Ellison can pull this off, in a short story at least, but the rest of us are going to need more than two characters, especially in a novel. A story's "supporting cast" is essential. You'll be pleasantly surprised by how fond of minor characters you can become, and how they can grow out of those roles to take on novels or even whole series of their own.

Drizzt Do'Urden, one of the genre's most popular characters, was first added to *The Crystal Shard* as a minor character at the suggestion of R. A. Salvatore's first editor, Mary Kirchoff. The actual hero of *The Crystal Shard* was a barbarian named Wulfgar. But more than twenty years later the whole series has been recast as The Legend of Drizzt, and a whole generation of fantasy fans couldn't imagine the genre without him. This doesn't mean you should approach supporting characters as potential heroes, looking to "better deal" your poor beleaguered hero. That happened organically with Drizzt, and it may happen again with one of your characters, but if you plan on it, all you're really doing is rethinking your hero. If your hero doesn't hold your interest, it's a reasonable certainty that he won't hold your readers' interest either. So do that thinking *before* you start writing.

In my capacity as an editor at Wizards of the Coast, I was working with bestselling author Troy Denning on his brilliant Forgotten Realms novel *Faces of Deception*. Midway through the first draft an ogre appeared out of nowhere and seemed to know the hero quite well. Troy attached a note to the manuscript assuring me that he would go back and add the ogre to the first half of the book in the revision. About halfway through he had realized he needed a new character. He was right, and the book is better for the addition. Like Troy, if you're writing along and feel that someone is missing, don't feel enslaved to an outline. Instead, explore that additional character, and don't be put off by the work of going back and putting him into the rest of the story.

WHAT THEY ADD

What do supporting characters do that's so important?

Comic Relief

A novel that is earnest and dark in every word of every sentence of every paragraph can be as hard to read as it is to write. In even the most grim fantasy there are moments of humor. Still, you should avoid having your hero or villain slip on a banana peel, drop his pants, or get hit in the face with a pie. Instead, create the court jester, the surly dwarf, or the pun-slinging starship engineer to do all of those things and more, providing a breather between life and death struggles of good versus evil.

A few words of caution: Avoid characters who serve no function other than to clown around. Just as the villain's plan requires solid motivation, the comic relief character's jokes have to come from the setting and serve the story. Too many random gags could be construed as you not taking your own story very seriously. We'll talk more about humor later, but for all characters, whatever their reason for existence, the three most important elements remain: motivation, motivation, and motivation.

Offer Sage Advice and Vital Information

Supporting characters can tell you all about the world.

"The emperor's son once killed a man in the streets of Giro City," the *wizard recalled, "because the man sneezed as the prince's carriage passed."*

Galen crumpled the sheet of parchment, breaking the prince's wax seal, and replied, "That man was my father."

This is better than:

Galen's father was killed by the impetuous prince, whose wax seal adorned the parchment he crumpled and tossed across the empty room.

Why? Because people talk to each other. It's easier and more compelling to read than paragraph after paragraph of exposition. Dialog is one of the things that makes a novel; the absence of dialog makes a textbook. Characters can tell each other an awful lot about the world in which they live, but again, motivation is the key.

If you're using dialog to cover setting details and/or move the story forward (and you should always be doing that), keep a sharp eye on the motivations of the characters in the scene. Why would the wizard tell Galen that story about the prince and the man who sneezed? Did he know all along he was talking about Galen's father? Was he trying to egg Galen on, hoping Galen will attack the prince, whom the wizard hates, to avenge his father's death? Is the wizard shocked to hear that Galen's father was a victim of the prince's ill temper? Does the wizard intend to warn the prince that Galen is coming after him?

What people say is secondary to *why they say it.*

Show How Monsters, Traps, and Magic Kill People

On the TV series *Star Trek* (the original one, with Captain Kirk and Mr. Spock), almost every week one or more crewmen wearing red shirts were horribly killed.

Why did *Star Trek* work its way through so many guys in red shirts? Because someone had to beam down with Captain Kirk and have all the salt sucked out of his body so that Captain Kirk (and we, the viewers) would have some idea what the crew was up against. Supporting characters are ready-made victims, but that doesn't mean you should spend their imaginary lives too cheaply. Even the guy who gets salt-sucked should be on the planet with the captain for a logical reason, have a name, and begin with some kind of connection to the hero, the villain, or both. The more we care about that guy in the red shirt, the worse we'll feel about his untimely demise, and the more worried we'll be when Captain Kirk is in danger of meeting the same fate.

KEEP THE COMPANY A REASONABLE SIZE

Supporting characters can bring more to a story than adding a little humor, providing some explanation of the world, and serving as convenient victims, of course, but keep an eye on the size of your cast. I've said before that if you're writing a novel, you don't have to worry about budgets for special effects, costumes, makeup, and set designs, so you can make the world as big as you like. Similarly, you have no budget for actors, so you could have a million extras in your giant throne room, and any number of characters with names and lines, oblivious to Screen Actors Guild contract stipulations. But that doesn't necessarily mean you *should* have a million named characters. Include more than a dozen and most of the time you're stretching readers' ability to keep track of who's who. Piling on the characters doesn't prove you're smarter. It's more likely to give readers the feeling that you're disorganized.

Do you need more than one comic relief character, or even one at all? Think carefully. If you have a wizened old Merlin/Gandalf-style wizard to dispense advice and information, do you need an alchemist, an innkeeper, and a beggar to do the same? Maybe. Perhaps Merlin knows all about magic, the alchemist can tell the hero what herbs to look for to cure the scalp-pox, the innkeeper knows who stole the Hammer of Kallian from the temple, and the beggar saw the princess sneaking out the back door of the brothel at dawn yesterday morning. But then again, maybe Merlin knows the right herbs, too, so no need for the alchemist. Keep asking those important questions: What does he know? How does he know it? Who else knows? Why would he—or why wouldn't he—tell the hero who stole the Hammer of Kallian? And so on.

CHAPTER 13

GIVE THEM VOICE

Though the way a character talks will be informed by your own authorial voice, you need to do some serious thinking about what each character sounds like. But don't be overzealous in creating colloquialisms and idioms for each character who expresses himself in dialog. The commonalities of expression can do more to make your setting come to life than anything else. It isn't always about how different they sound from each other, but how similar.

According to R. A. Salvatore, a character "might have a favorite saying or a few tell-tale quirks, but those things should be a logical outgrowth of who he is and how he thinks."

A character's identity—his place in the world, where he comes from, and his educational, racial, and religious background—all inform the way he speaks. But still not every white American who went to college sounds like every other white American who went to college. For instance, some people like to talk, and they will spend a hundred words where a more laconic character might answer with a shrug.

Legendary fantasy author Terry Brooks cautions, "Don't work too hard at trying to be different. Don't try to be someone you're not. Make the characters speak in voices that seem natural to you. Remember that much of what connects a reader to a character has nothing to do with voice. Much of it has to do with things like facial expressions and movement and character traits."

You've probably already had someone advise you to read your writing aloud, and this advice is particularly valuable when it comes to dialog. Does it roll off the tongue? Does it sound too formal or not formal enough? If it's funny, is this a character who wants to be funny, or are we laughing at his expense? If he's intentionally funny, he should be consistent. Remember, if he's a goofy dork now, he can't be scary later.

Speech patterns should also flow from the nature of the world. If you haven't yet determined if the emperor's court is highly formal, you won't know if people should speak in *thous* and *thees* and *shalts*. If you haven't selected the flora and fauna of the world, you won't know if people call each other *jackass*. What if there's no such thing as a jackass, but there is a gundrey, which is kind of like a monkey the size of an ox that people use as a pack animal. Maybe calling someone *gundrey* is like saying he's a big, dumb monkey?

This is a good example of skipping back and forth between the six steps, so take this advice to heart and come back to it when you're ready to bring your characters to life. Don't saddle yourself with a list of slang words and modify the world to accommodate them. It should happen the other way around.

To Sum Up

All of this can be best summed up by the words of Paul Park, author of *A Princess of Roumania* and its sequels: *The Tourmaline, The White Tyger,* and *The Hidden World.* I asked Paul, "What is the most important element to a richly realized character (his back-story, goals, politics/morality/ethics, family/relationships)? Where should an author start?"

Paul replied, "I often start by imagining the character as a physical and psychological object, and then imagining how that object appears to other people in the drama, including me. Then I start adding detail to justify or confound those assumptions. Then I go deeper, to see if I can discover an interior landscape that challenges the exterior one—in other words, how the character appears to him or herself. Then I invent a personal or family or romantic history that explains, or at least resonates with, those differences. Character motivation derives out of that process; it's not what I start with. But if everyone in the story knows the same things about a character, or imagines him or her in the same way as the author does, and there's no gap between what the character perceives and what the reader perceives, there's usually a problem."

Well said.

STEP THREE | THE WORLD

"Most fantasy landscapes are nostalgic in nature, dependent on a shared sense of history or myth. The interesting landscapes are familiar and unfamiliar at the same time."

—PAUL PARK, author of *A Princess of Romania*

World building is the one aspect of writing science fiction and fantasy that makes them more challenging to write than most other genres of fiction. A richly realized world is not more important than compelling characters, good writing, or creative, well-balanced action, but its creation can be more complex. We'll fall back on methods we've covered earlier, especially the idea of asking yourself an open-ended series of questions, giving yourself permission to work outside of a special effects budget and "think big," and so on. But we'll also talk a little bit about restraint, so you don't end up with an unrecognizable, overly complex setting no one can grasp.

Bestselling author Paul S. Kemp has some good advice on the subject of world building. "Don't get bogged down in it," he says. "It's an endless exercise. At some point, you have to tell a story, not get caught up in an encyclopedic exploration of the setting. Don't misunderstand, setting is incredibly important, but it's (with rare exceptions) just where things happen. It's the things that are happening and the characters caught up in those things that are more likely to enthrall readers."

CHAPTER 14

Decide on a Setting

"Characters are the most important piece of the fiction world," says J. M. McDermott, author of *Last Dragon*. "The world exists as your characters move through it. Focus on that interaction between the character and the place, and there you will find the sense of place you are desperate to convey."

Unless you're writing in someone else's shared world, the world you create is there to serve your story and characters, not the other way around. Keep in mind, too, that the word *world* can also mean an entire science fiction universe set in the far-flung future.

Before you start to build a world, decide on a setting. What's the difference between a setting and a world? Most of the time, those two words are used interchangeably, but it's fair to say that *setting* describes your basic approach, and the *world* you end up with is the result of layers of detail being added, like the layers of an onion, onto that setting.

TYPES OF WORLDS

Here are some varieties of worlds for you to consider.

Created Worlds

These are settings that are, not to put too fine a point on it, entirely *created* by the author. Robert Silverberg's Majipoor, for instance, previously existed in no other place and time but in Mr. Silverberg's imagination. Every city, every mountain range, every island was placed there by him, working, surely, from various sources of inspiration. The result is something that has never existed anywhere else before. Created worlds exist in science fiction as well, in one famous case preceded by these words: "A long time ago, in a galaxy far, far away."

Fantasized Worlds

This sort of thing results when an author takes a culture or nation out of the history of the real world and uses it as the sole or primary inspiration for a fantasy world. The Empire of Wa, for instance, in Sean Russell's *The Initiate Brother*, is a fantasized version of Imperial China. It isn't precisely China, but his cultural inspiration is clear in the naming conventions, customs, and so on. Though it may seem a subtle distinction, fantasized worlds are not the same as historical fantasy, though much of the same research will have to be done to create a fantasized China as would be done to set a novel in China itself. But with a fantasized world, the author takes much broader liberties with the source culture and history. Though it may be easy to assume that this is just a lazy version of historical fantasy, if done well, as with *The Initiate Brother*, it's no less rewarding a read as either an entirely created world or a richly researched historical world.

Historical Fantasy/Alternate History

These are novels set entirely in a real historical period, but they introduce fantastical or intentionally anachronistic technological elements. Susanna Clarke's seminal *Jonathan Strange & Mr. Norrell* is the gold standard by which all historical fantasies will be judged, and Harry Turtledove is the reigning king of serious alternate history. Clarke and Turtledove have set the bar high, so approach historical fantasy with care. Be prepared to spend many months, if not years, meticulously researching, and be prepared for detailed criticism if you get the slightest detail wrong.

Near or Far Future Science Fiction

This is really two categories lumped together. Near future science fiction is the hardest of the two to write because in order to make it plausible you have to be up on the latest trends in science and technology, and you *will* see your best efforts rendered obsolete in your lifetime. Arthur C. Clarke's *2001: A Space Odyssey*, for example, made utterly incorrect assumptions on the future of manned spaceflight. Far future science fiction affords the author much wider latitude, with a greater understanding on the part of the majority of readers that the author isn't actually trying to tell you what the world will be like in, say, the year 2552. The world created for the video game *HALO* is just fun to play in and read about while it speaks to contemporary issues of security, war, and xenophobia.

Contemporary (Urban) Fantasy and Science Fiction

What makes novels like Jim Butcher's *The Dresden Files* or Rachel Caine's Weather Warden series contemporary fantasies rather than thinly disguised horror novels is that the supernatural elements come from a character's ability to manipulate magic. Harry Dresden is a wizard who lives in today's Chicago.

The science fiction equivalent of contemporary fantasy assumes it's the here and now, but some kind of imaginary technology intrudes. Superheroes, UFO stories, and many mad scientist tales fall into this category. Michael Crichton was contemporary SF's true master, especially with books like *Jurassic Park* and *The Andromeda Strain*.

LET THE WORLD BUILDING BEGIN

Once you've chosen a basic approach, your world-building work starts. There are advantages and disadvantages to all of these categories, and choosing one or another, or combining them in whatever way your imagination allows, is an entirely personal decision. Historicals are hard, but there are drawbacks to the others as well. Created worlds are great when they work, like Tolkien's Middle Earth or Terry Brooks's Shannara, but the fantasy publishing battlefield is littered with the corpses of equally well realized worlds that failed to resonate with readers. Countless authors have had to come to grips with the fact that they've spent in some cases years creating a world they hoped would be the setting for a dozen books or more, only to hear their editors or agents say, "Maybe it's time for something new." When this occurs, the editor or agent is probably passing on a message that came from the community of science fiction and fantasy readers, who voted with their wallets.

CHAPTER 15
BUILD THE WORLD

"Know your world before you write," Terry Brooks cautions. "Have it clear in your mind."

Okay, then, let's dig in and really start working. You've settled on a setting—the overall approach. Now it's time to actually create the world by layering on details. But where to start?

The craft—the hard work—of world building can be boiled down to two elements: research and creativity. Before we get into specific factors like alien religions or how magic works in your world, some advice on research.

Research is a process of figuring out what to read. The Internet has made researching anything a lot easier and faster, but it can also be less authoritative. If you're creating, say, a fantasized version of pre–Columbian Mexico, you may not need to find the most authoritative sources. After all, you're creating your own version of that culture, so you'll want some details to come from your imagination. Still, better information is always better than worse information.

AVOID OVER- OR UNDER-RESEARCHING
Author Paul Park warns that "research can be a trap, a way to delay starting a book. I don't do a whole lot of general research; it's mostly on a need-to-know basis. After all, it's what you invent that will make your book original or derivative, and you can get started on that anytime."

True, but how much research you do as you build your world will depend on how closely related you want it to be to various real-world touchstones.

Your research will inform every step along the world-building process. Every chapter that follows in this book assumes you're doing relevant research along the way. In addition to getting your historical facts straight if you're writing the next *Jonathan Strange & Mr. Norrell*, research into the details of your world will help you balance plausibility and realism.

Studying historical events, languages, and customs can make you and your novel a lot smarter, but this is fantasy after all, historical or otherwise, so what readers want most from you is a glimpse into the deeper recesses of your imagination.

If you're writing a fantasized version of pre–Columbian Mexico, for instance, knowing the history of those cultures and their fascinating religious practices will ground it, but if there isn't some creativity, some special spark that makes it your own, why not just write a well-researched piece of historical fiction? Once you make one of these Aztec guys a wizard or awaken the feathered dragon of Xitchitxtchitl, it stops being historical fiction and becomes fantasy. Don't spare the imagination, even if you're grounding your world in the here and now or then and there, as opposed to a world of your own creation.

PLAUSIBILITY VERSUS REALISM

Realism is an important factor in historical and contemporary fantasy, alternate history, or near-future science fiction. If your contemporary wizard, like Harry Dresden, lives in Chicago, you need to go to Chicago. Breathe the air. Listen to how people talk. Make sure you know that they take the L to work, not the subway; that they drive on expressways, not freeways. Be sure to mention the pizza, too. It is an undisputed fact that pizza was perfected in Chicago. As were hot dogs.

In historical fantasy, you need to know when things like the electric light or the crossbow were invented and make sure that if someone in 1492 has a flashlight, it's part of the fantasy, not just a boneheaded mistake.

In created or fantasized worlds, all you need is *plausibility*, but that's no small thing. You have to clearly define a new set of rules germane to your world and stick to them. Fantasy and science fiction readers not only are willing to suspend their disbelief—they read those genres very specifically in order to do that—but also are hoping to experience a place where the impossible is possible. They want to inhabit, while they're reading your novel, a world rich in magic or the space-faring empires of the distant future.

Have fun creating your world, but take it as seriously as does international bestselling science fiction and fantasy author Kevin J. Anderson. "Doing the research and world building is the first step in developing the plot and characters," he says. "As I create the society, the history, the political structure, the geography . . . all those things lead to ideas for the story. I might develop part of a religion, which makes me think of a character, who becomes an integral part of a story." Again, be prepared to skip back and forth between steps.

CHAPTER 16
KNOW YOUR GEOGRAPHY

"Good stories, well told, are what matters," cautions Pyr editor Lou Anders. "Whether you obsessively build maps, or disdain them as Joe Abercrombie and M. John Harrison do, what you do in them is what counts."

But then, according to Kevin J. Anderson, his Terra Incognita books "are heavily driven by geography; the major conflicts flow from the locations of countries, of trade routes, of mines, deserts, ocean passages—I draw maps in detail and refer to them as I choreograph the plotlines."

MAPS ARE YOUR FRIENDS

Sketching out a rough map can help you remain logically consistent within your own world, with travel times that make sense and don't change, and with star systems or cities and other landmarks all in their proper place in relation to each other. You only have to tell your readers that the castle is eight miles north of town once for that to be fixed forever in space. Write that down on a map or in a note, remember where you wrote it down, refer back to it, and keep yourself and your world honest.

The balance of reality and fantasy, realism and plausibility, in your geography is entirely up to you. If you want the whole thing to be utterly bizarre, like a world that's really one giant tree, or a world inside a planet-sized whale swimming in an endless ocean, or something strange yet grounded in the fringes of science, like the exotic landscapes of Larry Niven's *The Smoke Ring* or *Ringworld*, go right ahead. If you'd rather take a more conservative approach and create a continent for your fantasy world that's not unlike Europe, then do that. A bizarre world doesn't automatically make you more creative, or a better writer. Truly strange worlds can overwhelm even a very strong story. Unless you intend for the world itself to be a metaphor for something germane to the story, like Ringworld, keep it simple.

RESEARCH YOUR MAPS

Some knowledge of the basics of geography can help you make your maps more plausible, and it can provide new ideas. Do you know where and why deserts form? Which direction rivers flow? Do you know why a certain part of a continent might be sunny and warm year round while another might have long, cruel winters?

If you spend some time learning how mountain ranges form and why they tend to cluster in certain patterns, if you understand where rivers begin and how they flow, if you know a little something about weather and the effects of geographical features on it, your map— your whole world—will *look right*, even if the overwhelming majority of readers would never be able to articulate what you did right and what you did wrong. If you skimp on the research, your readers will feel like something is off.

Look at political boundaries with the same critical eye. As you scan a reasonably detailed political map of the world, you'll find that there are very few straight lines. Political boundaries pretty much exclusively followed natural features like rivers and mountain ranges until very recently, at least in historical terms. One of the weird things about the United States of America is how many straight-line political boundaries we have, like the state of Colorado, which is actually rectangular. America is a young country, divided up by modern surveying techniques, and we were fairly civilized about parceling out land so that North and South Dakota didn't have to fight a war over where their state lines were drawn.

Skip to Chapter 25, which discusses available technology, and decide if your world has this sort of luxury. If not, the border between the Kingdom of Jarmon and the Ghringley Protectorate probably runs along something either side can defend, like a river or a mountain range.

CHAPTER 17

FILL YOUR WORLD WITH MONSTERS

You could probably find a science fiction novel, even a fantasy novel, that doesn't have any monsters in it, at least monsters in the traditional sense. Monsters aren't an *essential* component to every science fiction and fantasy story. But they are fun, and are as much a mainstay of both genres as anything else. The flying monkeys of *The Wonderful Wizard of Oz*, the beholders and mind flayers of *Dungeons & Dragons*, the beast that crawls through the darkness in Robert E. Howard's *"Red Nails," Dune's* mighty sandworms, the throw rug gone bad in the *Star Trek* episode "Devil in the Dark" . . . these are as much a part of our experience of the genres as wizards and starships.

WHAT'S A MONSTER?

It'll help if we settle on a definition. Charles Manson has been described as a monster, for instance, but is he? He's not a very nice guy and was responsible for horrifying acts of violence, but for our purposes, he's a *villain*, not a monster. He's not possessed of supernatural powers (regardless of what he may think), and despite being a violent sociopath he is as human as you and I.

A monster is any creature of a species that is neither a part of the civilization of sentient people or among the ranks of mundane flora and fauna.

I think we can generally settle on who is part of a civilization of sentient people. This means that if your world has a human kingdom, a gnome enclave, an empire of elves, and a city of zylvaani, and all these different types of humanoids (assuming zylvaani are humanoid) think of each other as a society of equals or sentient enemies, then gnomes, elves, and zylvaani aren't monsters.

We can easily define what "mundane flora and fauna" is, but you'll have to decide if all the mundane plants and animals of the real world also exist in your created fantasy world. Do people in that world ride horses, or giant beetles called ridgebacks because of the ridges on their backs? If these ridgebacks fill the same role as horses, they aren't monsters either, actually, since to people inside that world, who see them every day, a ridgeback is no more "monstrous" than a horse would be to us.

It's Different

An easier definition: *A monster is any animal you've never seen before.*

If you'd never been to a zoo or circus to see a lion in real life, never saw a picture of a lion, had never heard of such a thing, then were suddenly confronted by an enormous raging cat with massive claws and daggerlike fangs, you'd probably tell your friends about your encounter with, and narrow escape from, a monster: a giant cat-thing that looked at you as though you were a Happy Meal.

The human species has enjoyed a privilege that no other animal on the planet has ever attained, even the now-extinct Tyrannosaurus Rex: We are the apex predator in every environment on Earth. Some people are still killed by animals, sure, but it's a statistically irrelevant occurrence. In the so-called "Summer of the Shark," in 2001, five people worldwide were killed by sharks. That year at least fifty million sharks were killed by humans (some say as much as double that number). Encountering a lion out alone in the open savannah of central Africa would have to be a scary experience, but for the overwhelming majority of us, lions are curiosities we keep in zoos for the entertainment of our children. For all their inherent ferocity, sharks and lions are not monsters.

It's Scary

Here's a more specific definition of a monster: *A monster is something that tips the predator-prey scales on us, and is at least a* potentially *superior predator.*

In the case of living things that scare us—monsters—the idea of being hunted and eaten, of being treated like prey, works at a very primal part of our shared experience. We've created a world in which we can go on about our daily lives without worrying that we're being stalked by leopards. Wolves and some species of bears came perilously close to extinction at our hands, and the bestselling novel and blockbuster movie *Jaws* caused such a frightening spree of sport fishing for sharks, especially the great white, that author Peter Benchley campaigned to get people to stop killing them before there were none left. He showed us a "monster" living off our beaches and we responded like any predator whose territory is threatened: We went after it with all the weapons our evolution has provided us—fishing hooks, rifles, dynamite, and God knows what else.

THINK THROUGH YOUR MONSTERS

The question of whether or not to include monsters in your world and story is entirely your call, but if you do, approach the creation of new monsters and/or the inclusion of traditional, archetypal monsters (like dragons and unicorns) with as much care as you expend in placing mountain ranges on your map.

"First," according to Mike Resnick, monsters and aliens "have to fulfill the needs of the story. Second, I try to create monsters or aliens that are not quite what the reader is expecting. Mainly, I try to keep them from ever being considered generic."

If you do decide to use those mythological/fantasy archetype creatures like dragons and unicorns, make sure they are clearly *your* dragons and unicorns.

Anne McCaffrey created a rich culture of dragons for her Pern novels, which in part inspired the chromatic and metallic dragons of *Dungeons & Dragons*. Smaug the dragon from Tolkien's *The Hobbit* breathed fire and was red, and the red dragon of *D&D* is a nod to that seminal text, but the poison-gas-belching green dragon or the acid-spitting black dragon of *D&D* veers sharply away from Tolkien.

Restrictions to the type, size, shape, and capabilities of dragons in your fantasy world are limited only by your imagination. Fantasy readers like the archetypal tropes of the genre and expect to see them—they're what define fantasy as a genre, after all—but they're also very sensitive to what's been done before. Coughing up the same tired Smaug clone isn't going to set you apart. It will not help you find your voice, your world, or your own readership. Keeping in mind Mike Resnick's advice that your monsters must "fulfill the needs of the story," don't create a world full of monsters before you know at least in general terms what you want them to do in order to move the story forward.

The Monster as Metaphor

Monsters can serve as metaphors, like that funny rug-monster called the Horta in *Star Trek*'s "Devil in the Dark." In the beginning of the episode, harried miners call in Captain Kirk to save them from some kind of mindless, vicious monster that's been killing their comrades in the deep tunnels of a remote mining outpost. In the end it's revealed that the Horta is really a sentient being that's protecting a clutch of eggs from the careless miners. The monster serves as an allegory, a warning against the evils of poor resource and habitat management. If it was only an acid-spewing throw rug, we wouldn't still be talking about that episode more than forty years later. In that case, at least, the monster *was* the story.

Support the Main Character

Monsters don't need to be the primary focus of the story; but can fill supporting roles. The flying monkeys in *The Wonderful Wizard of Oz* were just particularly scary minions of the Wicked Witch. They captured Dorothy, and Toto too, but the story didn't hinge on their existence. One of the things that made the flying monkeys work is that even though the Wicked Witch had more mundane human guards whom she sent after Dorothy, the monkeys made the capture of Dorothy scarier, more dramatic.

Fantasy or science fiction writing often comes down to the act of *replacing things*: police or soldiers become squadrons of flying monkeys, the Horta takes the place of endangered animals displaced by "progress," and so on.

WHAT CREATURES ARE IN YOUR WORLD?

Do any or all of the animals we know from our own world also exist in your created world? Even if you're writing historical fantasy, it pays to answer this question. In this kind of fantasy, the answer's probably "yes," but what if you decided to write a historical fantasy set in Ancient Rome? Further suppose that the fantasy element—what makes it historical fantasy, and not just historical fiction—is that all of the animals we know today never evolved, but instead the Romans live alongside dinosaurs, or if not dinosaurs then a biosphere dominated by dragons. The setting makes it historical, and the dragons or dinosaurs make it fantasy. James Gurney did much the same in his popular Dinotopia series.

Flora and Fauna

The question of what defines mundane flora and fauna comes down to a choice between three solutions:

1. **This is a world in which all of the animals we know from the real world exist** (though we'll only see the ones appropriate for

the part of the world in which our story is set, so polar bears and leopards aren't mixed together). There are no monsters: no created animals at all.

2. **This is a world in which some or all of the animals we know from the real world exist** side by side with monsters and various created flora and fauna. Such is the case with the overwhelming majority of fantasy novels. For instance, there are both horses and monsters in Tolkien's Middle Earth and Moorcock's Young Kingdoms. If you decide to go this way, think through the reason why everyone knows what a horse is but people are surprised by the giant man-eating zix. Consider questions like these:

    • Where does the zix come from?
    • Is it just an animal that evolved on this world alongside the horse, or has it come to this world through a portal from the Dimension of Horrors?
    • If the zix is the size of Godzilla, evolved as part of the ecosystem of your world, and has a taste for flesh, why hasn't it eaten everything in the world by now?

Keep in mind that the animal kingdom resembles a pyramid, with a small number of large predators on the top and an increasingly large number of diminishingly small prey at the bottom. If every animal on an alien planet is a monstrous carnivore, chances are they all ate each other before your astronauts got there.

3. **This is a world in which none of the animals we know from the real world exist**, and absolutely everything has been replaced by created animals and monsters. These creatures often but not always fill the same niches that real animals fill, like mounts, draft animals, scary predators, and so on. Edgar Rice Burroughs's Barsoom (Mars) is a world filled with exotic created beasts, with no Earth animals at all.

This can be fun but a big commitment. If you opt to go this way, make the animal that fills in for the horse not just a giant beetle, but a giant beetle that does something a horse can't do, like walk up walls (since bugs can do that) or fly (like some species of beetles can do). Be prepared to keep extensive notes and refer to them often. If the beetle flies in one scene, it can still fly later on when you want them to be trapped on the mountaintop, so you'll need to address that somehow.

Science fiction authors don't really have to wrestle with this question. It's safe to assume that any alien planet surely will not have Earth animals on it, unless someone has taken specific action to bring them there. But science fiction readers will demand that some careful thought be put into the flora and fauna of an alien planet. Consider the conditions there. If the planet orbits a cool red dwarf star, for instance, chances are it's pretty cold on that planet. Animals will be adapted accordingly—they'll have fur or blubber to keep them warm, maybe wide feet to help them walk on snow, and so on. Make sure you set some rules for the alien animals' ecosystem, and be consistent with your application of those rules, while at the same time walking that fence between showing your readers what they need to see to keep the story moving forward, and trying to impress them with your extensive background notes.

CHAPTER 18
FILL YOUR WORLD WITH PEOPLE

In the previous chapter, I talked about a world in which humans, elves, gnomes, and zylvaani regarded one another as normal. That means we'll have to broaden our definition of the word *people*, which is generally used interchangeably with *human*. In a world that also includes societies of gnomes, elves, and zylvaani, it's entirely appropriate to specify that someone is a human, and that "elves are people too."

In more than one fantasy source, elves and humans are referred to as *races*. I think that's a bit of a misnomer, which makes it difficult to distinguish between humans of different races. I'm a human, and so are Oprah Winfrey, George Takei, and Fareed Zakaria, but we look a little different from each other, and we've called those differences *race*. It will be impossible to ignore racial distinctions if you're writing contemporary or near-future science fiction, or historical or contemporary fantasies, but you're entirely in control of the racial mix of the humans in your created world. And those distinctions do not have to be limited to humans. Thanks to the *Star Trek Voyager* character Tuvok, we know that Vulcans in the *Star Trek* universe come in at least two of the colors that humans come in. In our world, race has been a matter of conflict ranging from subtle, personal bigotry to outright genocide. It will be up to you to decide how different races of humans, different races of elves, and so on interact with each other. This can give your world an added layer of plausibility and allow you to opine on matters of racial politics.

DRAW SOME LESSONS FROM HISTORY

"A good trick for an author is to study human cultures and history," Kevin J. Anderson told me. "Learn the differences in our own sociology, and draw from those ingredients, exaggerate them, mix and match, and create something with a few familiar components and a few surprising ones."

This is true if you're creating a rich array of elves (a fantasy archetype) or zylvaani (a new fantasy or science fiction species). The archetypes tend to be obvious, drawn as they are from centuries if not millennia of folktales and legends. Elves, gnomes, dwarves, ogres, trolls, and so on are free for the taking, though as with archetypical monsters, you should make every effort to create an elf of your very own. The Keebler elves bear scant resemblance to the regal elves of The Lord of the Rings. Your elves should occupy, to the best of your ability, a third category.

Likewise, your aliens don't have to be Little Green Men from Planet X. Or, if they are, they should be Little Green Men who act differently from what the reader's come to expect.

This can be a difficulty when you decide to fall back on the archetypes. Kevin J. Anderson explains, "I try not to fall back on elves or dwarves . . . they tend to carry pointy things."

Ouch. But seriously, you have the whole history of myth and folklore to draw from, and centuries of fantasy and science fiction stories to inspire you—and to inform you of what has been done before. This is a good place to remind ourselves that anyone who wants to write in the fantasy or science fiction genres should also be *reading* those genres. If you're setting out to define your peculiar brand of dwarves, think carefully about how they compare to the dwarves in other fantasy novels you've read, and ultimately you will have to judge for yourself if you've created something you're excited about or if you're just carting out a cliché.

Mix and Match

As with monsters and flora and fauna, if you're starting with a created world, it'll be entirely up to you to determine the mix of sentient species and how many, if any, races are represented in each. It might be tempting, again as with monsters, to sit down and just start brainstorming so you end up with a dozen races of elves, three races of gnomes, five colors of zylvaani, the feyfolk, the unicorn-men, the merfolk, and three races of humans (all of whom hate each other) . . . on and on—but why?

"Why not?" won't quite suffice. Richly realized fantasy worlds full of color and detail can be great fun to create, and some have managed to resonate with readers for decades or longer, but they must be created with care.

How many races of elves do you need? To answer that you have to ask lots more questions: How different are they from each other? Maybe one race of elves has wings, another breathes underwater, and so forth, so basically there's an elf for every environment. That's fun. Are there civilized elves and wild elves? Why will that distinction matter? Will we ever meet all of these elves? Would it be better not to have aquatic elves *and* merfolk? How often is your story going to go underwater, even?

Some of this can be handled with the good old *casual mention.* A lot of world building comes from the occasional offhand remark: Someone refers to the winged elves, but we never meet one. We know they're there, but that superfluous reference only tells us that there are lots of different kinds of elves. Maybe in the sequel we'll finally meet a winged elf, and because of that casual mention in the first book, readers won't start wondering where these guys came from all of a sudden. This works best if you've made it clear why it's taken your hero this long to meet a winged elf: there are only a few left and they live in a remote part of the world, far from the human kingdoms.

What Do You Need?

Let the mix of species and races evolve with your story. What does your story need *right now*?

Comic relief: The zylvaani is a race of funny little guys that humans think are cute and hilarious.

The mentor: The zylvaani are a small group of creatures possessed of ancient wisdom who occasionally take on pupils.

The wise man: The zylvaani are an ancient, nearly extinct race of scholar-priests who live in the thin air at the top of the highest mountains where their monasteries hold all the mysteries of the universe.

Take your thinking a step beyond that. For instance, if your story needs wise men living on top of the mountains, why do they have to be zylvaani and not humans? Real-world humans live at startling altitudes and often go about their daily lives with no problem when visitors from the lowlands are dropping like flies from altitude sickness. If the wise men are zylvaani, there must be a reason. Dig deeper, and decide why there are both humans and zylvaani in your world and what makes them different.

In her Pern series, Anne McCaffrey eventually revealed that the humans on Pern were descendants of space colonists from Earth. Maybe the zylvaani evolved on your world and were nearly killed off by invading humans. Maybe the zylvaani are aliens from another planet or dimension. Maybe the zylvaani and humans share a common ancestry, like humans and Neanderthals.

You can spread this thinking as wide as you want. Possibly there are fifty different intelligent species on your world. What if animals from various environments on Earth had also developed the complex creativity needed to form language and technology, so that humans share the world with a fish civilization, a kingdom of intelligent birds, a lizard empire, and so on?

There will be lots more to consider in terms of species and race, which we'll cover as we discuss political systems, religions, and languages.

CHAPTER 19

TAKE US TO THEIR LEADER

If history has taught us anything, it's that people form groups to protect themselves from other groups. When the groups are very big and powerful, we call them "governments," but when they're smaller they have other names: corporations, families, syndicates, unions, special interest groups, charities, clubs, gangs, teams . . . .

You've started to do some thinking about the people of your created world, and the time has come to start dividing them into groups. These divisions can be as simple or as complex as your story calls for. Let's repeat that: *as your story calls for.* For the same reason you have to keep a reasonable eye on how many races of elves or space-faring pirate-raiders you have in your world, don't go nuts with political systems—unless you want to.

We're talking about individual imaginative choices. If it propels your story forward, makes a social or political point, or otherwise enriches the tale you have to tell, then by all means make your hero a member of a trade guild, a religion (though more on that one later), a secret society, a militia unit, a duchy, and an empire. Let's work our way backward through that example.

HE'S A CITIZEN OF AN EMPIRE
If you're like me and are honest with yourself, your identity as a citizen of the United States of America rarely intrudes on your day-to-day life. I'm not a politician or a lobbyist, nor do I serve in the military. If someone asks me my opinion of some point of national or international politics, I'll be more than happy to sound off, and

I may or may not be in agreement with whatever policies are being enacted or acted upon in Washington D.C., but I am not a policy maker. So what does being a citizen of this "empire," say about me?

I'm free to join a political party and run for office. I'm a citizen, not a convicted felon, and I have not been judged mentally ill (not been *judged*, anyway). I'm not a politician because I choose not to be a politician, just like I chose not to join the military. So if your hero is like me, and your story is smaller in scope, the empire may not ever really come into it—or will it?

I am writing this book in English because I was born in America. Had my grandparents decided to stay in Sparta, I would be writing this in Greek right now. I'm not religious, and that's at least in part due to the fact that I live in a country that, for the time being anyway, doesn't force me to adhere to a certain religion or meld cultural, racial, and religious identity like my Greek Orthodox grandparents' upbringing did. I'm firmly middle class, but compared to the average citizen of most of the sub-Saharan African nations I'm wondrously wealthy, so surely the fact that I'm an American tempers my socioeconomic reality and outlook. Does that mean that even if your book isn't about the hero actively saving the empire and becoming the emperor himself, or defeating the empire a la Luke Skywalker, the nature of the empire your hero calls home still matters? You bet.

Forms of Government

This is a good place to think about the way your fantasy government is organized. I've been using the word *empire* as an example, because it has a nice ring to it and has been used both in popular fantasy and popular science fiction, but that hardly means you have to start with an empire. Do some research into political science, at least enough to look up the definitions of this partial list of forms of government:

- anarchy
- mercantilism

- democracy/republic
- oligarchy
- feudalism
- dictatorship/totalitarianism
- communism
- confederacy/federation

You can combine these with each other and further modify them with any number of the following:

- geriatocratic
- patriarchal
- matriarchal
- militaristic
- plutocratic
- theocratic
- magocratic

Does your hero come from a theocratic oligarchy (a nation ruled by a closed group of religious leaders) that's facing off in a world-spanning war against a magocratic confederacy (a coalition of smaller nation-states ruled by wizards) while a geriatocratic republic (a nation ruled by elected officials who are all senior citizens) tries desperately to engineer a peace treaty?

More Inspiration from the Past
Look back through history for examples of governments that fit into these categories, test the boundaries, and create categories of your own. Could your world contain an elvocracy (only elves are allowed to hold power)? How about a patriarchal, theocratic republic (in which only male members of one particular clergy can be elected to parliament)? It's yours to decide.

Mike Resnick has drawn ideas from history, but he has a much bigger bag of tricks. "Of course there are other sources," he says, "and the more unusual and the less-used the better. I won the Prix Tour Eiffel [and he was the only American, the only English-language writer to win it] for my novel *The Dark Lady*, told in the first person of an alien whose entire society was extrapolated from the matriarchy and herd instincts of the African elephant. Which is to say: source material is *everywhere*, and if you don't just look where everyone else is looking you're more likely to create something unique and memorable."

HE'S A CITIZEN OF A DUCHY

Using myself as an example again, I'm a citizen of the "duchy," or *state*, of Washington. I became a citizen of the state of Washington when my job was moved two thousand miles west from Lake Geneva, Wisconsin, where I worked while actually living in Schaumburg, Illinois . . . and I was born in Rochester, New York.

Culturally speaking, Washington isn't really a lot different from Illinois—the pace is a little slower, maybe, and aside from a slight shift in accent and a completely unfathomable desire to be Green Bay Packer fans, Wisconsin is even more like Illinois. But some states are substantially different from one another. Louisiana and New Hampshire are at least as different from each other as, say, France is from Germany.

So if you take the time to tell the reader that your hero comes from a particular duchy, make that duchy at least as different from the other duchies as Louisiana is from New Hampshire. If they're more like Illinois and Wisconsin, why do you need that division? What does it add to the story?

If the Duke of Illinois and the Baron of Wisconsin are brothers who hate each other and the two duchies are at war, with the emperor remaining neutral for some reason, then which duchy your hero belongs to will matter even if the cultural differences between those two duchies are few. Do what moves your story forward.

HE'S A MEMBER OF A MILITIA UNIT

So he's loyal to the—which? Empire? Duchy? Neither? Maybe he lives in a duchy within an empire and hates both the evil duke and the really evil emperor, so his militia unit is really a group of freedom fighters condemned as traitors by their own government. Maybe each duke is required to raise some number of troops, so each town has a separate militia and the hero is perfectly happy to march off to war in defense of duke and emperor. If neither is the case, don't bother with the militia—unless that's the reason why your hero knows all these really cool spear-fighting moves even though when the book starts he's just a simple farmer: he's a simple farmer who spent some years in the militia. That's a good reason to tell us he's a militiaman, even if we never see him march off to war with the militia.

HE'S A MEMBER OF A SECRET SOCIETY

What does this secret society do, and how does being a member make your hero more heroic? Is it a social club, like a fantasy version of the Kiwanis? Or is he a member of the Fraternal Order of the Flaming Skull, keepers of the Tome of the Allmind, leaders of which have entrusted him with a page from the tome that he must memorize so if the last copy is ever destroyed it can be recreated by the thousand members, each having memorized one of the tome's thousand pages? What does the Allmind have to say about the world that will move your story forward?

If all you can tell us about this cryptic tome is that a thousand people are memorizing it, and it has nothing to do with the story besides "adding color," then please take a moment to collect yourself and jettison the Order of the Flaming Skull. But if the evil Duke Blagojevich of Illinois is systematically killing the thousand devotees of the Flaming Skull in order to wipe the words of the Allmind from the memory of mankind, that sounds like a story is forming.

HE'S A MEMBER OF A RELIGION

We'll talk about religion in more detail later, so set that aside for now.

HE'S A MEMBER OF A UNION OR GUILD

What do occupation-based organizations do in your world? In Frank Herbert's *Dune*, the Spacing Guild maintained complete control of travel between the stars. In an empire comprised of far-flung planets orbiting distant stars, that control made them as powerful as the emperor himself. Is your hero, the simple farmer/militiaman, a member of the farmer's guild? The spear-fighters guild? Is his guild affiliation just a cover for his activities as part of the Fraternal Order of the Flaming Skull? If you can't answer these questions with something that moves your story forward, dump the union.

To Sum Up

Author Kevin J. Anderson says he's often inspired by history. He recommends that authors should "study histories other than America or England. Japan, ancient China, Maori, Russian . . . they are rich in legends, events, rulers, scandals, tragedies, heroic battles, wars. All of those things can provide inspiration, even a template, for a new story."

Your world is not an end to itself. The setting is there to propel your story forward and make your characters richer. If you're doing any sort of world building that doesn't function in both of those capacities, you're wasting your time and your readers'.

STEP FOUR | DETAILS

"Like our own world, a fantasy setting is layered with themes, histories, inhabitants and cultures. Like the smith who turns various ores into steel, we must add these elements in just the right amounts until our visions take shape and eventually develop life of their own."

—LOGAN MASTERSON, *Fantasy Magazine*

You might be starting to wonder if the process of world building is endless. It may seem as though there are too many things—an infinite number of factors—to keep in mind. But heed the basic advice at the heart of all of this: keep yourself firmly planted in the minds and needs of your characters. There is an awful lot you'll need to know about the science fiction universe or fantasy world those characters inhabit, but don't let yourself get off track and start world building without a purpose. The purpose of a novel is to tell a story through the actions of its characters.

And the process is not infinite. It's easier tackled if you think in terms of broad categories, such as those that follow.

CHAPTER 20
WHEN IN ZYLTARIIA . . .

Bestselling author Kevin J. Anderson offers this advice on the subject of creating cultures: "In my Saga of Seven Suns I created the Ildirans, which are (on the surface) fairly human but have dramatic cultural differences as you get to know them. Over the course of seven volumes in the series, I explored and enriched that race, unfolding one more detail after another. A race has to have a certain shared basis with humanity, or they will be too distant for the reader to relate to."

An excellent place to start. Different people have different patterns of behavior, different social expectations, a different idiom, colloquialisms, table manners . . . . If you're creating a world from the ground up, those cultural peculiarities will be yours to invent. If you're working in a contemporary, near-future, or historical setting, get your research cap on.

This can be the hardest part of world building. Governments are fairly easily categorized, religions may be copied from the rich history of human mythology and superstition, and maps can be redrawn from real-world sources both contemporary and historical. Cultures can also be re-imagined from the real world. But more than anything, the cultural "upbringing" (for lack of a better word) of your characters—hero, villain, and supporting cast alike—has the biggest effect on how real, how sympathetic, and how *plausible* they and your world are.

In the previous chapter we touched on the relative difference between Illinois and Wisconsin as an example of how subtle the differences between political subdivisions can be. But consider the differences and similarities between two English-speaking nations: the United States and Great Britain.

A quick list:

- The British have a parliament, Americans have a Senate and House of Representatives.
- The British have a prime minister, Americans have a president.
- The British have a foreign secretary, Americans have a secretary of state.
- The British drive on the left, Americans drive on the right.
- The British buy things with pounds and weigh things in stone, Americans buy things with dollars and weigh things in pounds.

How much do all of those things matter? The difference between the foreign secretary and the secretary of state is a matter of semantics—but semantics matters. In your fantasy world, is there a *foreign secretary* or a *minister of barbarian affairs*, because the evil empire thinks everyone who doesn't live in the empire is a barbarian? See how that job title tells us something about the empire?

When it comes to answering the question of "What do I call it?" you may be surprised by how much your decision will tell readers about your world's culture. If the emperor has a foreign secretary, the title doesn't tell us much, but when we see the foreign secretary planning the genocide of the gnome population of Zyltariia, we start to wonder: Is this what foreign secretaries do, or is this particular foreign secretary overreaching? If this guy holds the title Minister of Gnomic Eradication, he's just doing the job the emperor hired him for, isn't he? If you chose to be subtle and simply call him the foreign secretary, then you're telling us that the empire has things to hide, and perhaps that when the post was first formed, it had a less evil agenda.

Of course, if you give someone the official title Minister of Gnomic Eradication, we also know that the empire is openly racist against gnomes, and entirely unashamed to be so.

DEFINING CULTURE

Before we go any farther, let's make a list of a few things that define a culture—or more accurately, *help* define a culture, since in all fairness no culture can be defined by one thing.

- religion
- colloquialism/idiom
- weights and measures
- diet/cuisine
- music, art, and pop culture
- nationalism and individual liberty
- prejudice/racism/tolerance
- manners

A pretty short list, but it'll keep us busy for a while. The first three we'll tackle in the chapters that follow, but let's spend a paragraph at least on the rest of the list now.

Diet/Cuisine

How many times have you asked friends, coworkers, or family, "What does everyone want for lunch—Mexican, Chinese, or Indian?" Clearly we're talking about three distinct cultural traditions here. On the other hand, it's a stretch to discern the precise difference between Polish and Russian cuisine. My wife is Polish-American and we live in an area where there's a large immigrant population from Russia, so there are plenty of Russian restaurants that serve all sorts of stuff she grew up eating as "Polish food." In contrast, the difference between Polish food and Japanese food, say, is huge.

Some cultures don't tend to identify as strongly with their cuisine as do, say, the French and the Italians. Their regional dishes are matters of extraordinary nationalistic pride. Not only what people eat, but *how* they eat it—with forks, their hands, chopsticks— *when* they eat, and where they eat, can be of vital significance to a culture.

If the evil galactic empire eats meat while the rebel folk indigenous to the swamp world of Darvon are vegetarians, that might piss off some meat eaters among your readers. But don't be too afraid to piss people off. You're going to do it anyway.

Remember that scene in *Indiana Jones and the Temple of Doom* where the heroes are confronted with the horrifying spectacle of eating monkey brains? That was fun. Or the scene in *Galaxy Quest* when one of the characters is presented with a bowl of what appears to be live leaches? Yum. Weird food can be used for fun and effect, and it can also be a way for characters to communicate with each other. If the custom in Zyltariia is to offer a guest in your house a piece of fruit, and our heroine is not offered a piece of fruit when she visits her ex-boyfriend's new wife, then she has just received a message. That's the kind of detail that can move a story forward, using customs to show readers where the characters stand in relation to each other and the plot.

Music, Art, and Pop Culture

These can be difficult to portray in prose form—music especially— but it can be done, and I encourage you to try. Here's a line that tells us a little about Galen and how he feels about being in Zyltariia: "The discordant cacophony of the Zyltariian orchestra stung Galen's ears." He hates the music, anyway. But is it really "discordant," or is Galen just prejudiced against Zyltariians? Use these details if his reaction to the music moves your story forward somehow. Otherwise, it's fine to say only that there's an orchestra playing; that still sets a scene and tells us we're someplace special. Maybe it lets us know that the owner of the house is wealthy enough to afford an orchestra. Perhaps orchestras are routinely hired for ceremonies during which someone is sacrificed to the fire god, and Galen had no idea there was going to be a sacrifice until he saw the orchestra. Now the presence of the orchestra isn't just window dressing but a call to action. Can Galen rescue the sacrificial victim before the evil deed is done?

Describe the Art of the World

Art may challenge your powers of description, but anything worth doing is worth doing well. Most cities in our real world tend to look more or less the same now, but a lot of what makes Paris Paris, for instance, is the richness of its architecture. The Eiffel Tower has become a symbol of the city.

The Trevi Fountain in Rome isn't just a public waterworks project. People travel a very long way to see the Statue of Liberty: a work of art with enormous cultural meaning. When the Taliban blew up the giant Buddhas of Afghanistan's Bamiyan Valley it was a crime not just against the Buddhist philosophy but against the entire human race. What does that act tell us about the culture of the Taliban? What does the extent to which the Greek government is going to preserve the Parthenon tell us about Greek society?

The Importance of Popular Culture

When the Berlin Wall came down, what did East Germans do first? Well, most of them visited with long-separated relatives, but then they went to McDonalds, bought Rolling Stones CDs, and went to the movies. A cogent argument could be made that one of the reasons the Soviet Union failed was because it cut its population off from popular culture. How we're entertained tells us a lot about each other. Time and again it's been the popular artworks that have lived on the longest. In five hundred years, a historian who really wants to know what it was like to live in America in, say, the last twenty years of the twentieth century, should read Stephen King, Danielle Steel, and Tom Clancy—for the same reason we still read William Shakespeare, Charles Dickens, and the fantasy adventure story *Beowulf.* The religion you've created for your world, or the pomp and circumstance of official ceremonies, will tell us what the people of that culture aspire to, but what makes people laugh, or what they think is pretty or "cool," will tell your readers more about what it's really like to live, day to day, in that strange new world.

Nationalism and Individual Liberty

These don't always go hand in hand. Some societies have exhibited jaw-dropping degrees of nationalist fervor while utterly eradicating (or trying to, at least) all sense of individual liberty—Cambodia under the Khmer Rouge in the 1970s, for instance.

The expectations of the people about personal liberty within a particular culture go a very long way toward helping to define how your characters behave—and what makes them different.

Captain Kirk is obviously only tenuously interested in the United Federation of Planets, quickly and casually defying direct orders up to and including the Prime Directive, while at the same time maintaining a purely objectivist self-confidence. The *Enterprise* is "his" ship, not Starfleet's. That tells us volumes about this character. No one has to say out loud: "Captain Kirk is a self-centered non-patriot who's so good at his job that the government leaves him alone to do with the galaxy as he damn well pleases."

Prejudice/Racism/Tolerance

How a culture balances these issues will also drive a character and plot. Part of what makes R. A. Salvatore's Drizzt Do'Urden so popular is that he comes out of the Underdark into a world that instantly hates him because of the color of his skin. He's a dark elf, and dark elves have become synonymous with evil, so the above-world people perceive Drizzt as evil, too. How he changes first his own mind then causes the people around him to change theirs has been resonating in a very special way with readers for the twenty-plus years that Salvatore has been writing about this character.

Racism is still the hottest of the hot-button issues in America today, so it's not something to deal with lightly. If you create a culture in which there is an endemic racism against gnomes, you have begun to write a novel about racism. That issue will have a tendency to eclipse any other point you're trying to make. By all means, proceed with a novel that delves as deeply into that subject as you're intellectually capable of, but proceed with the utmost caution.

Manners

These aren't as much fun as cool stuff like plasma weapons, stardrive technology, and evil death cults, but even if you don't sit down and think about manners before you start writing, your work will be infused by them. Don't limit your thinking to the hyper-formalized systems of manners that you might encounter in Victorian parlors. A simple problem like how people greet each other will raise its head in your writing.

Do they say *hello, well met,* or *greetings? Live long and prosper?* Do they shake hands, salute, or kiss? And of course there's more.

When they sit down to dinner, do they start ripping into suckling pigs with both hands, or do they all wait for the baroness to start eating first? Do men and women walk hand in hand in the street, or would such a wanton display of lust mean prison terms for them both? Is it rude to burp, kiss, sneeze, or ask "How ya doin'?" Is it polite to fart, smile, bow, or ask "In what way may I serve?"

The fast way through all this is to adopt a system of manners and protocol that you're comfortable with. It's fine if people in your fantasy world approach each other in more or less the same way that we do.

On the other hand, you may want to tilt your world a little more toward Victorian, or Persian, or feudal Japanese cultures. All of these were more strict, more formal, more ritualistic than we tend to be today.

We haven't made it to education, law, access to power, economic opportunity, sexual mores . . . the list is almost endless, but we have to stop somewhere, so how about this?

In an essay first published in 1940 entitled "The Lion and the Unicorn: Socialism and the English Genius," George Orwell described English culture in 1940:

> But in all societies the common people must live to some extent *against* the existing order. The genuinely popular culture of England is something that goes on beneath the surface, unofficially and more or less frowned on by the authorities. One thing one notices if one looks directly at the common people, especially in the big towns, is that they are not puritanical. They are inveterate gamblers, drink as much beer as their wages will permit, are devoted to bawdy jokes, and use probably the foulest language in the world. They have to satisfy these tastes in the face of astonishing, hypocritical laws (licensing laws, lottery acts, etc., etc.) which are designed to interfere with everybody but in practice allow everything to happen. Also, the common people are without definite religious belief, and have been so for centuries.

He continues:

> One can learn a good deal about the spirit of England from the comic coloured postcards that you see in the windows of cheap stationers' shops. These things are a sort of diary

upon which the English people have unconsciously recorded themselves. Their old-fashioned outlook, their graded snob-beries, their mixture of bawdiness and hypocrisy, their extreme gentleness, their deeply moral attitude to life, are all mirrored there.

If you can write a couple of paragraphs like that about your created world, you're headed in the right direction.

CHAPTER 21

DEFINE A SYSTEM OF WEIGHTS AND MEASURES

Authors of contemporary or urban fantasy or near-future science fiction don't generally have to spend much time suffering over systems of weights and measures. If you're writing the story of a wizard in present-day America, time will be measured by days, weeks, months, and years; distance by inches, feet, and miles; weight in pounds; and money in dollars. If your science fiction story is set a few decades in the future, it's unlikely that we'll have redefined our system of weights and measures much if at all—even if the United States adopts the metric system.

If you're writing historical fantasy, weights and measures can become a big research topic for you. You'll have the challenge of depicting a society that measures distance in, say, cubits, and you must make that understandable to a contemporary audience. If you're writing in a created fantasy world, far-future science fiction, or science fiction in which the dominant culture is alien, you might be tempted to create a system of measures all your own. Before you do that—before you do anything—some words of caution. I will put them in italics so no one can say I didn't emphasize it strongly enough:

If you're translating everything your characters do and say from their native language, either real-world foreign, historical, or created, choose with the utmost caution what you choose not *to translate.*

For instance, if a centon is the same as a minute . . .

MAKE TIME THAT MAKES SENSE

In the old *Battlestar Galactica* television series from the late seventies, our heroes are humans who have been separated from the rest of humanity and are on a pilgrimage to find what has for them become the legendary Earth. It's naturally assumed that though the actors are speaking English, their characters are speaking their own native language, and they've got their own system of weights and measures. To emphasize this point, the characters say "Wait a centon" instead of "Wait a minute."

I'm sure there are hardcore fans out there who will find my opinion sacrilegious, but I believe that was a terrible decision. If a centon and a minute are essentially the same, why not translate *centon* into *minute* and get on with telling the story? No episode was improved by the fact that they worked in centons instead of minutes.

And please heed this advice: Never, in any science fiction story, put the word *Earth* before a unit of measurement:

"I give you five of your Earth minutes to surrender." It sounds silly.

If you're dead-set on creating your own units of time, make them mean something. It's statistically impossible that any planet revolves around its sun at *exactly* the same speed Earth does, so an alien planet your characters visit will have a longer or shorter year than we do. In science fiction you must address this, but in a created fantasy world a year can be identical to Earth. Why not?

Whatever you do, do it for a reason. Do it to make a point, to move your story forward—not just because.

WHEN IS A CUBIT NOT A CUBIT?

The same considerations apply to units of distance such as inches, centimeters, feet, cubits, yards, meters, leagues, miles, kilometers, light-years, and parsecs. If it *matters* that a distance is "three cubits long" and not "four and a half feet long," then okay. Otherwise, leave it in normal measure.

GRAMS, POUNDS, KILOS, OR STONE

You have to decide how much things weigh—grams, pounds, stone, kilograms, tons—and my advice remains the same: Common real-world measurements always trump invented units unless it really matters. If a character is told by an alien that something weighs three *bloons*, he might think that doesn't sound like much, then be surprised that a *bloon* is equivalent to fourteen thousand pounds. In this case you're having fun with the confusion between different systems of measurement—it's making your story better somehow. Do that, but if your hero already knows that a *bloon* is fourteen thousand pounds, so no one is surprised or inconvenienced by it, then for the sake of your readers' sanity, please just say they have to move 42,000 pounds of cargo and get on with the story.

HOW MUCH DOES IT COST?

In our own world most countries have their own currency (the exception is the Euro), so readers tend to associate a certain currency with a particular place. If you're creating an alien culture, it will seem weird if the aliens pay for things in dollars. Near and even far-future science fiction can certainly still use dollars, or yen, or Euros—but even then if one of those currencies has achieved dominance over the others, that could tell us something about your vision of the near future.

For historical settings, you'll need to research currencies, but unless commerce is a huge part of your story it'll rarely be necessary to help your readers with conversions. If a character in your early Roman period historical fantasy—or time-travel SF novel—pays a single *as* for a loaf of bread and doesn't find that particularly cheap or expensive, then that's all we need to know. An *as* isn't a lot of money. For created currencies, assume that most people—most Americans anyway—will think of a million units of currency as a lot, a billion a really lot, and one not very much.

It may sound as though I've just advised you not to create your own units of measure, and for the most part I've done just that. But at the same time, I encourage you to let your imagination run free. Just be sensitive to the readers who will have to chase after it.

CHAPTER 22
SPEAK THE LANGUAGE

In the previous chapter I stressed the following piece of advice:

If you're translating everything your characters do and say from their native language, either real-world foreign, historical, or created, choose with the utmost caution what you choose not *to translate.*

Kevin J. Anderson agrees. "I will sprinkle strange alien words or expletives, new terms that convey the alienness of a concept," he says, "but as a writer—the teller of the tale—I am translating the dialog into the written word. In English. It always reads clumsy to me when characters speak in stilted, overly foreign words. They're speaking their own language and it should sound as normal to the reader as it sounds to the character. It's part of the suspension of disbelief."

If you've been reading science fiction and fantasy for a while, you've probably encountered books with too many made-up words or you've been confused a few times. But strange names for characters and places is part of the allure of fantasy and science fiction, isn't it? Who wouldn't much rather read about Elric of Melniboné's journey to Nadoskor than Jim's trip to Toledo—even if he's going to Toledo, Spain, instead of Toledo, Ohio? It's the exotic hero in an exotic world that we show up for.

But as with changing minutes to *centons*, proceed with caution and always with an eye on *what makes your story better.* By all means, make up names for people, places, and things, but choose carefully what you want to translate from Zyltariian to English, be consistent, and consider the bigger picture.

AVOID OVER-LAYERING

To illustrate this point, here's a paragraph from an imaginary fantasy novel. You'll see that though adding exotic detail helps, too much can become overwhelming and drag down your story.

DRAFT ONE

Bronwyn stared up at the imposing silhouette of the king's castle. The walls, made of rough-cut granite, were thirty feet tall, and from the shadows at the edge of the Hindrid Forest, she watched as a pair of guards slowly made their night rounds, appearing and disappearing between the battlements. Both were elves, like their king, but unlike Bronwyn they were red elves—more like the dwarves in surliness and general ill humor. As she waited for them to disappear into the watchtower she considered the climb. Her pack weighed almost seventy pounds, so she would need to leave it behind. If anyone happened upon it in the night—and bandits were common enough in the Barony of Gildé—all they'd get away with was maybe a few gold coins' worth of camping supplies and beef jerky. And in the case of the jerky, she thought, good riddance to bad company. She shrugged the pack off and strung one of the arm straps around the low-hanging branch of a maple tree, though she doubted that would keep the raccoons out. She wanted to bring her lute with her—that was worth more than a few gold coins—but she knew she'd have to leave it behind. She had to get in and out of the castle in less than an hour, or she'd never make it back in time to save her mother's life.

Pretty clear, but other than the name Bronwyn, the name of the forest, and the name of the barony, it's written in plain English, with very little else besides references to archetypal fantasy critters (elves and dwarves) to make it "fantasy." We could make this paragraph more exotic and interesting, so let's start searching and replacing.

Back in Chapter 17 we talked about created worlds in which every single animal is imagined, where no real-world flora or fauna exists. If this sample story was set in that world, it would read like this:

DRAFT TWO

Bronwyn stared up at the imposing silhouette of the king's castle. The walls, made of rough-cut karnstone, were thirty feet tall, and from the shadows at the edge of the Hindrid Forest, she watched as a pair of guards slowly made their night rounds, appearing and disappearing between the battlements. Both were elves, like their king, but unlike Bronwyn they were red elves—more like the dwarves in surliness and general ill humor. As she waited for them to disappear into the watchtower she considered the climb. Her pack weighed almost seventy pounds, so she would need to leave it behind. If anyone happened upon it in the night—and bandits were common enough in the Barony of Gildé—all they'd get away with was maybe a few gold coins' worth of camping supplies and beef jerky. And in the case of the jerky, she thought, good riddance to bad company. She shrugged the pack off and strung one of the arm straps around the low-hanging branch of a sipplewood, though she doubted that would keep the chitterbits out. She wanted to bring her lute with her—that was worth more than a few gold coins—but she knew she'd have to leave it behind. She had to get in and out of the castle in less than an hour, or she'd never make it back in time to save her mother's life.

I'm assuming that at some point previous to this we've established what a chitterbit is. The fact that castles are built out of karnstone tells us that karnstone is probably a pretty hard material, and it's clear in context that a sipplewood is a kind of tree. But what if we also want to avoid archetypal character species and races? We'll need to get rid of those elves and dwarves. And if there are no cows in this world, how can she be carrying beef jerky?

DRAFT THREE

Bronwyn stared up at the imposing silhouette of the king's castle. The walls, made of rough-cut karnstone, were thirty feet tall, and from the shadows at the edge of the Hindrid Forest, she watched as a pair of guards slowly made their night rounds, appearing and disappearing between the battlements. Both were jinarrions, like their king, but unlike Bronwyn they were red jinarrions—more like the rockfolk in surliness and general ill humor. As she waited for them to disappear into the watchtower she considered the climb. Her pack weighed almost seventy pounds, so she would need to leave it behind. If anyone happened upon it in the night—and bandits were common enough in the Barony of Gildé—all they'd get away with was maybe a few gold coins' worth of camping supplies and milliak jerky. And in the case of the jerky, she thought, good riddance to bad company. She shrugged the pack off and strung one of the arm straps around the low-hanging branch of a sipplewood, though she doubted that would keep the chitterbits out. She wanted to bring her lute with her— that was worth more than a few gold coins—but she knew she'd have to leave it behind. She had to get in and out of the castle in less than an hour, or she'd never make it back in time to save her mother's life.

Prior to this scene, we would make clear the difference between a red jinarrion and whatever color of jinarrion Bronwyn is. Even if this is the first mention of the rockfolk, at least we now know that they tend to be surly and of general ill humor. And we fixed that pesky beef thing. Whatever a milliak is, it must be an animal eaten by jinarrions, so that might be all we need to know about milliaks, too.

Here's where some authors start slapping on too much detail. Let's add a system of weights, measures, timekeeping, and currency, each painstakingly detailed in a thirty-page appendix at the end of the novel.

DRAFT FOUR

Bronwyn stared up at the imposing silhouette of the king's castle. The walls, made of rough-cut karnstone, were thirty sixth-hoons tall, and from the shadows at the edge of the Hindrid Forest, she watched as a pair of guards slowly made their night rounds, appearing and disappearing between the battlements. Both were jinarrions, like their king, but unlike Bronwyn they were red jinarrions—more like the rockfolk in surliness and general ill humor. As she waited for them to disappear into the watchtower she considered the climb. Her pack weighed almost seventy ninety-weights, so she would need to leave it behind. If anyone happened upon it in the night—and bandits were common enough in the Barony of Gildé—all they'd get away with was maybe a few Ravenstones' worth of camping supplies and milliak jerky. And in the case of the jerky, she thought, good riddance to bad company. She shrugged the pack off and strung one of the arm straps around the low-hanging branch of a sipplewood, though she doubted that would keep the chitterbits out. She wanted to bring her lute with her—that was worth more than a few Ravenstones—but she knew she'd have to leave it behind. She had to get in and out of the castle in less than a multicon, or she'd never make it back in time to save her mother's life.

In the creation of this world, we've been devising a rich fantasy culture in which there are various sorts of bandits. Some are steal-from-the-rich-give-to-the-poor types, others are like land pirates, and others are racist mobs who only target purple jinarrions. Your extensive notes say that the most common bandits in the Barony of Gildé are the gold-hungry Apostles of St. Alexandra. A couple pages later in your notebook is the part where we decided that just calling a king a king and a guard a guard was boring so we made up a whole system of ranks for our political and military organizations. Oh, and we also decided that it's boring to have real-world musical instruments, even period instruments. Bronwyn is a prodigy on the julyun, which is like a lute but with half the number of strings.

DRAFT FIVE

Bronwyn stared up at the imposing silhouette of the imperator general's castle. The walls, made of rough-cut karnstone, were thirty sixth-hoons tall, and from the shadows at the edge of the Hindrid Forest, she watched as a pair of corrinnions slowly made their night rounds, appearing and disappearing between the battlements. Both were jinarrions, like their imperator general, but unlike Bronwyn they were red jinarrions—more like the rockfolk in surliness and general ill humor. As she waited for them to disappear into the watchtower she considered the climb. Her pack weighed almost seventy ninety-weights, so she would need to leave it behind. If anyone happened upon it in the night—and the Apostles of St. Alexandra were common enough in the Barony of Gildé—all they'd get away with was maybe a few Ravenstones' worth of camping supplies and milliak jerky. And in the case of the jerky, she thought, good riddance to bad company. She shrugged the pack off and strung one of the arm straps around the low-hanging branch of a sipplewood, though she doubted that would keep the chitterbits out. She wanted to bring her julyun with her—that was worth more than a few Ravenstones—but she knew she'd have to leave it behind. She had to get in and out of the castle in less than a multicon, or she'd never make it back in time to save her mother's life.

Whew! We haven't even talked about idiom yet, but we should. Every culture has its turn of phrase, its common metaphors, its figures of speech. In Bronwyn's world, the Garrians were a race of barbaric humanoids who were fond of raping and pillaging everything they happened upon. So Bronwyn grew up around people who were fond of the saying "Wave good-bye to the Garrians," which means, "Good riddance to bad company."

A few more missing elements. The word *castle* is so been-there-done-that. We want to stress that the imperator general lives in something more fitting his importance, like a star citadel. A sixth-hoon is actually 8 inches long, and a ninety-weight is the weight of 90 newborn babies, so that's about 720 pounds; round it down to 700, so 70 pounds is really a tenth of a ninety-weight, and the walls are actually 22.5 sixth-hoons tall.

Bronwyn's people hold to a sort of "it takes a village" custom when it comes to raising children, so every woman in the village was technically her mother. The woman she's saving was the woman in whose house she slept, which makes her Bronwyn's night-mother.

Here's our final version:

DRAFT SIX

Bronwyn stared up at the imposing silhouette of the imperator general's star citadel. The walls, made of rough-cut karnstone, were twenty-two-and-a-half sixth-hoons tall, and from the shadows at the edge of the Hindrid Forest, she watched as a pair of corrinnions slowly made their night rounds, appearing and disappearing between the battlements. Both were jinarrions, like their imperator general, but unlike Bronwyn they were red jinarrions—more like the rockfolk in surliness and general ill humor. As she waited for them to disappear into the watchtower she considered the climb. Her pack weighed almost a tenth of a ninety-weight, so she would need to leave it behind. If anyone happened upon it in the night—and the Apostles of St. Alexandra were common enough in the Barony of Gildé—all they'd get away with was maybe a few Ravenstones' worth of camping supplies and milliak jerky. And in the case of the jerky, she thought, wave good-bye to the Garrians. She shrugged the pack off and strung one of the arm straps around the low-hanging branch of a sipplewood, though she doubted that would keep the chitterbits out. She wanted to bring her julyun with her—that was worth more than a few Ravenstones—but she knew she'd have to leave it behind. She had to get in and out of the star citadel in less than an multicon, or she'd never make it back in time to save her night-mother's life.

Go back and read the first draft of the paragraph again. Then read that last version one more time. Any one or two of these layers we added in the drafts made the paragraph more interesting to read. All of them together made it a terrible mess.

IS THIS GOOD FOR YOUR STORY?

Paul Park notes that he tries to "shy away from invented vocabulary, which tends to sound bogus to me. It only works if you take the trouble to invent an entire language, as Tolkien did."

Consistency in naming things can be a tough job, and different authors have taken different paths to achieve the illusion of a foreign language. The science fiction role-playing game *Traveller* had random word-generator tables. By rolling dice and referring to a complex series of charts you ended up with nonsensical words that had certain sounds in common. It was fascinating, really. If you want to come up with something like that, please do. Other authors have referenced real-world languages, though that assumes your readers won't recognize, say, Hungarian swear words.

Combine Words to Form New Ones

Sometimes it's helpful to combine mundane words to create new forms. Take Skywalker, for instance, an evocative name made from two ordinary words. Study the pages of baby name books, looking for names that mean something. In a created world, the names for people and places will be entirely yours to choose, so pick something you can live with if you're lucky enough to still be writing about that character or place twenty years from now.

And one last bit of advice: Say it out loud. Don't wait until you have to read it for the audio book producers to find out it's unpronounceable.

CHAPTER 23

RENDER UNTO GORTHAK WHAT IS GORTHAK'S

Authors of both science fiction and fantasy have long been concerned with the subject of religion. Novelists have written from points of view ranging from the outright atheistic all the way through to the evangelical. It's a subject that can rarely be ignored. For good or ill almost every human culture has had a religion at its core, though some cultures have replaced religion—the belief in a supernatural/superhuman entity or entities—with something more accurately referred to as a philosophy—a system of ethics based entirely on human behavior.

If you're going to write historical, contemporary, or near-future settings you will have to make some careful decisions about real-world religions. Most often your initial choice of a time and setting will determine what role religion plays in your story. If you set your story during the Salem witch trials, you've just taken a big bite out of the American Puritanical apple, so to speak—likewise with such periods as the Crusades, the Spanish Inquisition, or the Holocaust. Each is a time when religion was used as an excuse for brutality, but you could alternately find a time and place in history where religion had a calming, civilizing, charitable effect and run with that. The Left Behind series took evangelical Christianity to a sort of SF/fantasy extreme, against the backdrop of the rapture. The writer L. Ron Hubbard used science fiction to create a religion of his own, Scientology.

Researching religions both contemporary and historical is a worthy pursuit for any author, though if you're writing the farthest of far-future science fiction you may imagine a post-religious society. Religious questions may be a driving force in a novel set in an alternate history setting—one, for instance, that attempts to answer the question: "What if the Roman Empire never embraced Christianity and instead Europe maintained its polytheism into the twenty-first century?" In such a scenario, how could you imagine the way in which the absence of Christianity might have changed Europe if you don't understand the effect Christianity actually *had* on European history?

DRAW ON THE REAL WORLD

As with all else, feel free to find inspiration in real-world religions, as author Kevin J. Anderson did in his Terra Incognita trilogy. His story "is driven by a clash between two opposing religions—Aidenists and Urecari—based on Medieval Christianity and Medieval Islam." Anderson says, "I studied both of those base religions and the historical context, then adapted them, created my own symbols, the different priesthoods, the rituals, then extrapolated them into the society. For a religion to be believable, it has to extend outside the bounds of the church or temple and into the daily lives of the people."

Religion need not overwhelm a story or characters. The deeper an understanding of it you have, the more naturally it will fit in as a part of your fictional world's backdrop. As you ask yourself questions about your created religion, you'll start to wonder how it affects your characters. There may be simple, day-to-day things—do characters start every morning with a prayer?—or complicated, larger events, such as when your hero rescues a would-be victim of human sacrifice.

In far future or entirely imagined science fiction universes the subject of religion can be avoided a bit or glossed over, but it doesn't have to be. In British author Simon R. Green's space opera series that began with the novel *Deathstalker*, there's a faction known as the Church Militant. These are religious zealots—one part Spanish Inquisition, one part al Qaeda, and one part Moral Majority—who serve as pawns for villains and foils for heroes. Green spends no words at all putting the Church Militant's dogma into any kind of context. They're just violent religious fanatics. For his purposes, that's enough, and the Church Militant works in the context of the series and his created far-future universe.

THE ROLE OF RELIGION IN THE STORY

Some authors, like Frank Herbert, expend a lot of thought on the role of religion in the world and in their story, and it informs much of what progresses as the story unfolds. Kevin J. Anderson notes, "One of the best examples, to me, is what Frank Herbert created in *Dune* with the Fremen and their belief in Shai-Hulud. On the surface, it might seem a typical 'primitive people worshiping a giant monster' as you see in so many clichéd fantasies. But the Fremen have an entire accompanying philosophy, that the sandworms aren't really the god but a manifestation of the power of the desert; they have water rituals (which stem directly from the harsh desert landscape in which they live); they have a culture surrounding their religion: prayers, common sayings, all the details that show how pervasive those beliefs are."

Religion doesn't just give you a list of rules. There's a lot more to the Judeo-Christian playbook than the Ten Commandments. Religion sinks tendrils into all aspects of daily life from the obvious, like saying grace before eating, to what has become—in our culture at least—the mundane, with expressions like "Oh my God" or "for God's sake," not actually meaning to invoke the deity—they've become simply figures of speech.

As Kevin J. Anderson points out, there's more to a well-crafted imagined religion than a series of idiomatic search-and-replaces ("Oh my Gorthak," or "for Gorthak's sake"). The religion of the

Fremen in *Dune* comes out of the environment in which they live. If you've created a religion for a science fiction novel set on a planet that is as much a body of water as Frank Herbert's Arrakis was a desert, how would the water-world people's religion differ from *Dune*'s? Historically, people tend to build religions around things they need, dangers they face, or knowledge they're missing. Religion fills a need. Before you go off creating sacrificial rites and exotic rituals, think carefully about what the people of your world *need* from their gods.

WE'RE BACK TO ASKING QUESTIONS

That same advice again: Ask questions that inspire more questions, and keep asking and answering until you feel you've got something. When do you know you've "got something"? One clue may be when you spend the better part of a day thinking about it and can't come up with another question. Or if God appears and tells you to get off your ass and start writing.

CHAPTER 24

IT'S NOT FANTASY WITHOUT MAGIC

As with every aspect of world building, when you are devising a magic system, consistency is king. For example, let's say you write a scene in which your hero, a wizard, conjures a ball of purple fire that engulfs an entire village, but a hundred pages later, he watches in impotent horror as a marauding gang of bandits storms down a hill. "Now wait a minute," alert readers will say. "Why doesn't he just conjure up that purple fire and immolate the evil bandits?" If he does conjure up that fire, it had better be purple again or readers will need to understand why it isn't purple—is it a different sort of magical fire? If there's no fire, then you'll need to make clear why he's unable to conjure it up in this instance when he could before.

The same problem would occur if these two scenes were reversed: if the wizard could do something on page 200 that he couldn't do on page 20. If he's gained an ability to generate purple fire, you *must* show us how he learned to do this in the intervening 180 pages.

NOTES ARE YOUR FRIEND

The greatest aid to consistency is to *take notes*. If you know how magic works and have it written down somewhere, problems like this can be avoided.

If you're writing in a shared-world setting like the *Dungeons & Dragons*–related novels or *World of Warcraft*, the game gives you a detailed system of magic. Take that seriously or your editor will take it seriously for you. But even without a predetermined system of magic at your disposal—and *D&D*'s rules (or those from *World of Warcraft*, or *Warhammer*) are something authors of those novels should embrace and accept as inspiration, not combat as strictures—you'll need to be just as consistent with your own created magic system as you would be with someone else's.

Keep your notes on your computer, or your notebook by your side, and refer to them often. Read back carefully, and think about how magic infuses and affects every scene. If your wizard can teleport with the snap of his fingers, why is he trapped in a cave a couple chapters later? Don't forget what your magic does, how it does it, and who can use it.

Do some serious thinking about how "magic rich" you would like your world to be. Is this a historical setting in which a little magic might go a long way? A world in which magic is rare and banned for its dangerous unpredictability, or highly prized for its power and exotic rarity? For instance, in Robert E. Howard's Conan stories, magic is rare, generally considered a bad thing practiced by witches and necromancers, and Conan tends to react to it with fear and revulsion. But in Philip Pullman's *The Golden Compass*, everyone, even little kids, has a dæmon familiar, and no one thinks this is at all strange

Again we find ourselves at the crossroads of realism and plausibility.

Magic is pretend. In the real world it doesn't work. That means any fantasy novel you read (or write) is instantly unbelievable—it is inherently *unrealistic*. But that's what we love about fantasy. We don't want it to be realistic. We'll leave realism to Nelson Algren, Harvey Pekar, and other Quotidians. At the same time, this doesn't mean your story can go off on whatever flight of fancy comes to you in the moment and still be a well-crafted work of fiction.

CONSISTENCY IS THE FATHER OF PLAUSIBILITY

If the wizard can conjure a storm of purple fire, we don't believe that could actually happen in real life—which would make it *realistic*.

But if he conjures the fire in the same way every time, if the spell follows its own proscribed set of rules, we accept that it happened in the context of that fantasy world—we find it *plausible*.

On the other hand, if the purple fire is suddenly ten times more destructive in Chapter 14 than it was in Chapter 3, and you give no thought to making clear why or how it's more powerful, it's less plausible, and you'll start to lose your readers, you'll upset their suspension of disbelief. But suppose the wizard picked up a purple crystal along the way that seemed to pulse with magical energy, and the next time he conjures his purple fire he's surprised to find it's bigger and more destructive. The reader then understands that something new has been added: the crystal somehow supplements the wizard's purple fire.

MAKE MAGIC SERVE YOUR STORY

Unless you're designing a game, there's no reason to start by explaining how magic works and then forcing your characters and story into that scheme. As with all other aspects of world building, magic must first and foremost *serve your characters and story*, moving them forward rather than holding them back.

When Paul Park began thinking about his breakout novel *A Princess of Roumania*, he "did a certain amount of research into the history and technology of alchemy, and then imagined that alchemy actually worked. The magical procedures in the books were derived from scientific procedures."

He did research. He read up on the subject. There are numerous sources on the history of magic, from scholarly anthropological studies to "New Age" self-help books. Pick and choose from these, keeping in mind that the human animal is infinitely creative, and over the millennia we've come up with some wild stuff from zombie potions to pyramid power, crystal vibrations to astrology. The history of occult and religious practices, myth and legend, will offer up a Vegas-sized buffet of inspiration.

Take all that, then, and make it your own. Though individual creativity is essential in all things, in the fashioning of a magic system a little bit more inventiveness than the last guy will go a long way. Read extensively, then think. Ask questions again, always with an eye on your characters and your story. What will the way magic works tell your readers about your characters and the world in which they live? How will magic move the plot forward? Then think carefully about the effect that magic will have on your world.

In 1962's "Profiles of the Future," science fiction legend Arthur C. Clarke wrote, "Any sufficiently advanced technology is indistinguishable from magic."

I'll bring that up again in the next chapter when I talk about technology, but let's turn that around in the context of fantasy: *Any sufficiently advanced magic is indistinguishable from technology.*

Magic is a tool. It may be a rare tool useable only by a chosen few, or it may be something almost everyone has access to and uses casually in daily life. Does the conjured purple fire in our ongoing example replace the flame thrower or a napalm bomb? When it's used as a weapon, yes. A crystal ball or magic mirror used to communicate over vast distances is a fantasy version of the telephone. The Oracle of Delphi and Google serve the same function, don't they?

When Alexander Graham Bell first invented the telephone, there were only two of them. Had he stopped there it might have seemed like some kind of magical device. This would be the magic mirror of a low-magic world. Maybe there are only two in existence in the whole world, used by the evil queen to communicate with her general who's sailing out to attack the island of the elves. But once the telephone was marketed and mass produced, and eventually everyone had one, it certainly seemed a lot less magical, but the world itself also changed in very real, very dramatic ways. The modern fire department grew out of our ability to quickly call the operator, then 911, to summon help from a distance. Whole industries were born, from pizza delivery to phone sex. So if in your world everybody has a magic mirror they can use like a video phone, make sure you think that through in terms of how quickly characters can communicate with each other. Writers of contemporary action movies now have to contend with the cell phone, for instance, and they often go to great lengths to somehow isolate their characters in a time and place where very few people are ever truly isolated.

CHAPTER 25

IT'S NOT SCIENCE FICTION WITHOUT TECHNOLOGY

In the last chapter we discussed magic systems in the context of fantasy, and it may seem then that this chapter is germane only to science fiction. Ah, if only it were that simple. *Technology exists in any story in which the protagonists are creatively intelligent beings.* A caveman with a sharpened stick is making use of the cutting-edge (pun kinda intended—sorry) technology of his day. A sea elf defending himself against a kraken with an enchanted trident is doing the same, as is an interstellar marine hefting the latest model fusion blaster. A technological item is anything that anyone *makes*, especially tools.

MORE RESEARCH TO DO

In determining your world's available technology, you'll want to do some research and ask yourself more questions, but how deeply you delve into either the history of medieval metallurgy or the inner workings of the Large Hadron Collider is really up to you. Your fantasy world, if it's entirely created, doesn't have to be an accurate reflection of any real-world time and space, and slipstream or broadly drawn space opera doesn't have to rely too heavily on scientific and engineering journals. Acclaimed science fiction author Mike Resnick, for instance, describes himself as "kind of the anti–Arthur C. Clarke." He admits that he puts in "a lot of thought and very little research. I never want the technology to be the star of the story or to distract or divert from the human story I want to tell."

On the other hand, authors who decide to delve into historical fantasy, alternate history, contemporary science fiction or urban fantasy, or near-future science fiction are going to have to be prepared to do quite a bit more research. If you're determined to go down that route, either you've already done a lot of the digging or you're the kind of person who sees research as a fascinating challenge. If you possess an excess of intellectual curiosity, research stops being a drag, and the only problem you face is knowing when to stop studying and start writing.

THE FIVE CATEGORIES OF TECHNOLOGY

For simplicity's sake I've broken all of technology down into five broad categories, though I freely admit there are lots more, and a reasonable person may combine two of mine into one, and so on.

Weapons

Some people complain that science fiction and fantasy are inherently violent genres, overly concerned with macho wish fulfillment expressed as armed violence as the primary means of conflict resolution. My first published fantasy novel, *Baldur's Gate*, began with this sentence: "The blades came together so hard they threw out a blue-white spark bright enough to burn its gentle arc into Abdel's vision." So, I suppose I could be accused of feeding into that stereotype. In fact, there are plenty of science fiction and fantasy novels that aren't overly preoccupied with violent action and weaponry. But for those that are . . .

Fantasy Weaponry

Fantasy weapons usually start at a basic medieval or early Renaissance technology level: swords and armor, catapults and trebuchets, mounted cavalry, and maybe very early cannons. In that case you should get a sense of the variety of blades and pole weapons, and the accuracy of things like the bow and arrow or the javelin. Medieval and ancient archers tended to act more as artillery—their bows were indirect fire weapons that sent a cloud of arrows over the enemy's line. One archer rarely targeted a particular enemy soldier. A minute ago I mentioned the catapult and the trebuchet—do you know the difference? Does it matter? Is one arrow enough to kill someone? Could you survive even one hit with a battle-axe? Read and make notes until you have an answer.

Study the effect of one technology on another. Did the invention of the crossbow change the way armor was made? The invention of the musket sure did. The cannon made walled cities obsolete, didn't it? What good is a wall if your enemy can easily lob bombs over it from a distance or siege engines can blow a hole in it? In a fully invented world, don't be afraid to mix and match or invent weapons. Combine magic and technology to make things that were never seen in real life, like machine-crossbows or flaming swords.

Are Blasters Better than Swords?

Science fiction weapons should be no less well considered. Does your future world have laser weapons? If so, how do you defend against them? What is a "blaster," actually? You don't have to write a patent application for one, mind you, but if it can melt a hole in a starship's bulkhead in Chapter 3, it can do it again in Chapter 8. Just as with the magical purple fire, consistency and plausibility rule in the realm of technology, and you should be making no fewer notes in order to keep a strict eye on your own rules.

Architecture

Set aside the obvious: fantasy novels have castles and science fiction has starports. Building technology has changed an awful lot over the course of human history, and cultures from the Ancient Greeks to the oil-rich billionaires of present-day Dubai have expressed themselves in architecture. Some places—from the classical architecture of London or Paris to the stately row-house neighborhoods of Philadelphia—take an austere, pragmatic view of building. Other cultures—whether European aristocrats or Long Island's *nouveau riche*—spend a couple extra million bucks in order to make a building knock your socks off.

The Egyptians and other ancient cultures built pyramids because in an era before the invention of the steel crane, the ziggurat or pyramid was the easiest shape for a very tall building. Even the grandest of the pyramids was little more than a pile of stone blocks, with stepped or slanted sides your workers could walk up as they went along. As impressive as the Great Pyramids are, I think the average Egyptian pharaoh would be blown off his feet by one glimpse of the Sears Tower's 1,400 feet of vertical glass and steel. What does that mean to your fantasy or science fiction novel? What sort of buildings your world has (temples, bathhouses, public schools) will tell us about the culture of its people, and the size and shape (squat ziggurats, magical walking huts, anti-gravity floating cities) of their buildings will tell us about their available technology.

You can tell your reader a lot about the setting of your story by how people live in it. Medieval technology allowed for some impressive buildings, but there's a reasonable limit to how tall a brick building can be before it collapses under its own weight. You really can't build a building the height of the Sears Tower with anything other than steel—or magically infused bricks, or stone mined from the Quarry of the Gods, or the wood of the nine-thousand-foot-tall sky-reach trees of the Forest of the Primal Ones. Especially in fantasy, don't limit yourself to medieval materials if you don't have to. What a building is made of can tell a story, too.

What wonders does the future of materials processing have in store for the architect? A space elevator that stretches all the way to orbit? A space station so huge it forms a continuous ring around the Earth? Thinking even bigger, what about Larry Niven's Ringworld, a world so huge it stretches around a sun? What about a Dyson sphere that actually *encloses* a star?

If people in your far-future universe live in little two-story brick houses, that tells us something about that time: that somehow, for some reason, technology stopped and reversed, either because of some disaster or because people rejected the unchecked advance of technology and purposely ushered in a new era of simplicity.

Vehicles

In his tales of John Carter of Mars, Edgar Rice Burroughs imagined fantastic flying machines that carried his hero and his Martian princess around the world of Barsoom. And Burroughs was just the beginning. Fantasy has given us vehicles from flying ships to witches' broomsticks, and flying mounts of all species, sizes, and shapes. Even if you start with a medieval level of technology, your created world doesn't have to be limited to horse- or ox-drawn carts. Couldn't those carts drive themselves via magic, so they're like enchanted automobiles?

The first submarine brought to bear in a real-life wartime mission was the *Turtle*, invented in 1775 by American David Bushnell and set to work to bear (with mixed results) in the Revolutionary War. In your fantasy world inventors may have perfected the submarine long before they achieved other eighteenth-century technologies. Just as you did with magic, think through the greater implications of vehicles. If there are fliers, are there thousands or even millions of them? Are they like cars: almost everybody has one? Or are there a scant handful of expensive, exotic, experimental prototypes that only the emperor maintains?

How Fast Do They Go?

How quickly, conveniently, and economically people travel will determine how spread out their cities are. It also affects how quickly help can arrive when your hero gets in trouble: An hour? A minute? A month?

Science fiction vehicles can range from mundane cars with a twist, like the flying cars of the movie *Blade Runner*, all the way up

to *Star Wars*'s Death Star. Remember the reaction of Obi-wan and
Luke Skywalker when they first realized that the Death Star was
man-made? They were freaked out and impressed, even had a hard
time believing it at first. That told us a lot about those characters and
how in over their heads they felt—how small they seemed in the face
of that massive symbol of Imperial might. And we instantly knew
that the Death Star was something special, something new.

Likewise, the *U.S.S. Enterprise* was as much a star of the various
Star Trek series than any of the human (or Vulcan, or Klingon) characters. Not only were its mission and crew defined, but as the series
progressed we got a better and better view of the ship's capabilities.
The writers also tried, to the best of their ability, to be consistent
with its capabilities. The phaser beams always came from the same
place at the bottom of the saucer section, and the shuttlecraft never
came out of anywhere but the little garage in back.

Science fiction vehicles must be consistently handled in order to
be plausible. If you know how warp drive works, stop wasting your
time writing science fiction novels and get thee to a patent attorney
as fast as humanly possible so you can begin enjoying your reign as
the Bill Gates of faster-than-light travel. If you're not sure exactly
how your starship breaks the light speed barrier, don't fear, just set
your own rules and stick to them. Your readers have bought a science
fiction novel so they *get* that you made it up. But please let them
know that you're paying attention to your own creation. If it takes
three hours to get from Earth to Alpha Centauri, it takes three hours
to get back.

Information Technology

We all think of "information technology" as the latest 3G phone
or the next computer operating system upgrade, but there was
information technology in ancient times. Stone tablets carved with
Cuneiform inscriptions were examples of information technology.
Gutenberg's printing press was a huge leap forward in communica-
tions technology. Fantasy and science fiction authors need to con-

sider how people communicate with each other over distance and/ or time.

Has someone invented the printing press in your world? Are there schools for anyone but the privileged few? Are average people literate? Before the printing press, hand-copied books in Europe were tremendously expensive, so the overwhelming majority of Europeans in the Middle Ages never owned a book.

Let's go back and say your story includes magic mirrors that act as telephones. Do they have something like 3G capability? Can they record conversations, allow you to eavesdrop on remote locations, or let you listen in on someone's thoughts? If they can do any of those things and everyone has one, how has society adapted?

Two of the biggest questions facing the science fiction author about information technology are:

- Is there artificial intelligence?
- Can people communicate by faster-than-light means?

Answering the first question will determine whether your robots (if any) will become frightened when confronted by threats, like C-3PO does, or react to stimulus in a pre-programmed way, even if that programming sometimes goes off kilter. True artificial intelligence means that your computer/robot is as much a creative, emotional being as any human. If your robot can think for itself but is unable to form an opinion about whether or not it's a slave, it's a machine. If it can feel exploited, it's a person. Arthur C. Clarke dealt with this in *2001: A Space Odyssey*, as did Isaac Asimov in *I, Robot*.

For the purposes of your science fiction story, you do need to spend some time thinking about how people communicate with each other and their computers. Computers are not going to go away (unless you're writing a post-apocalyptic story) and they're going to continue to get more sophisticated. Do they plug into your head like in William Gibson's seminal *Neuromancer*, or do they answer back when you speak to them like in *Star Trek: The Next Generation*?

If you're writing a story set in a future where people are able to travel faster than light and begin exploring or settling far-flung solar systems, decide if their communication technology has caught up to their speed of travel. For most of human history communication was limited by the speed that someone could carry a message. The invention of the telegraph, and the telephone soon after, was world-altering in that it allowed real-time conversations between distant points. But what happens when you travel faster than light but you're still using some version of radio, which continues to be confined to Einstein's universal speed limit? That means if you phone home from Alpha Centauri it takes four years or so for someone on Earth to hear the phone ringing and another four years or so before you hear them say hello. But if you're talking on something like the subspace radio from *Star Trek*, that boundary is broken. Consider the various implications then decide that for yourself, based on the needs of your characters and your story.

Mundane Stuff

Residents of a medieval-level society spent an awful lot of time doing very ordinary things that we zip through with hardly a thought in the twenty-first century. Being a housewife in the Middle Ages was hard work. There was no running water, let alone a washing machine. The men tilling the fields certainly weren't riding around in modern combines, listening to the radio in air-conditioned comfort. The progress of human society can actually be traced by the distance between the calories required to produce food versus the calories taken in. This doesn't mean that medieval people were skinnier than we are, necessarily, but they worked a lot harder for every calorie than we do as we pop TV dinners into the microwave.

Think about magic in your fantasy world—how pervasive it is, how mundane, and its effect on day-to-day technologies. Do people cook with magic ovens that prepare the meal from a bag of vegetables and a live chicken? Have they invented a magical refrigerator? A toaster powered by bound fire elementals? And how does all that change the way people interact with the world? And why does it matter to your story that someone can have toast for breakfast?

Most technological advances in human history have been driven by one of two things: convenience or war. Vacuum cleaners and washing machines made it unnecessary for even very rich people to employ armies of servants. Strangely enough, over the years we've developed our self-reliance through a dependence on modern conveniences. Will this trend continue into the future? I don't know, and neither do you, but you don't have to be able to see into the future to write plausible science fiction. You only need to look into your imagination, carefully craft your own set of rules, and follow them for plausibility's sake.

To Sum Up

Remember: If you're translating everything your characters do and say from their native language, either real-world foreign, historical, or created, choose with the utmost caution what you choose *not* to translate.

Always keep in mind that your book should be readable. You don't get points for complexity alone. Tell your story first, and build the world to serve your characters, not the other way around.

Don't spend any time suffering over whether or not your book is realistic—if it's science fiction or fantasy, it isn't—but suffer a lot over whether or not it's plausible. Plausibility is built from consistency. Set your own rules, and once you've set them, follow them.

As always, ask questions, and find your answers by digging through research into history, current events, engineering, occult practices, religion, architecture, ancient and cutting-edge technology, and so on. If you're creating a world of your own, really make it your own. Remember, you have no special effects budget when you're writing a novel, so let your imagination soar. Let your world be as big as you can imagine, as long as your characters are big enough not to get lost in it.

Know when to say, "Enough!" to research and explanation. Heed this advice from veteran fantasy author Terry Brooks: "Three-quarters of what you know about that world should never appear in your book, but you should be able to speak to it, anyway. Your writing should suggest to the reader that if he thought to ask you, he would discover that you know a lot more than you're telling him."

STEP FIVE | NUTS AND BOLTS

"Fantasy is the genre where reality is only the starting point, and the imagination takes over from there."

—KEVIN J. ANDERSON, coauthor of *Paul of Dune*

There are three essential elements of the craft of genre writing: action, romance, and humor. All three will inform the characters you've started to develop, color the plot of your novel, showcase your unique world, and help express your idea or theme. The balance between these three elements will also help define the subgenre you're working in, and it will inform your publisher's efforts to market the book. As with all aspects of fiction writing, or any art or craft, practice makes perfect. You can find advice on writing an exciting action scene here and in other books, but there's no formula you can follow that will make you an immediate success. Take this advice to heart and keep banging on that keyboard. If writing is truly where your talents lie, in time you'll find what works for you and what doesn't, and eventually you'll have a book in which something happens in an interesting way.

CHAPTER 26

DON'T SPARE THE ACTION

In fantasy and science fiction, the word *action* probably conjures up visions of steely eyed warriors locked in mortal combat, blade-to-blade, *mano a mano*. Or maybe a single hero desperately fending off the hungry assault of a hideous monster straight from some madman's nightmare. Or a valiant ragtag group of colonists fending off an advancing horde of alien shocktroopers with only their farm tools and maintenance robots to protect them.

But open that definition up a bit and you'll find that there's a little bit of action happening all the time. Though those action set pieces are essential to any successful science fiction or fantasy novel, so are the little action sequences that occur within every single scene.

BUSINESS

As I'm typing this, at the desk in a little loft space in the upstairs hallway at home, my son is passing back and forth from the stairs engaged in various work-avoidance strategies to put off the inevitable homework. My wife is downstairs doing something I can't see, but I can hear her moving around down there. Wait—the dog just barked. My daughter is even now asking me for some paper from the printer. The television is on, but I don't think anyone is watching it.

All this counts as action. My son walks by reciting TV commercial catch-phrases. He's moving. He's doing something. And he's doing it for a reason: He doesn't want to do his homework. So like everything, his "action" is motivated. In the movie world they call this kind of thing "business."

The pages of a screenplay might contain lines of dialog alternating between two or three characters, but if those people are just volleying lines back and forth, it'll feel pretty dull on screen. That's why conversations in movies and television shows tend to take place while characters are walking along the beach, eating at a restaurant, or digging through a kitchen cabinet looking for something. And if the movie is well written, there's a *reason* for them to be there as opposed to someplace else, doing that as opposed to something else.

If three of your characters are in a room and all they're doing is batting about dialog, you may be moving the story forward, but you're doing so in a limp and lifeless way.

Sometimes you can express as much in carefully crafted action, including smaller actions ("business") as you can in dialog.

DIALOG ONE

"Bronwyn couldn't have survived the fire, your highness," Galen told the king.

"I know. And I know you loved her very much, but if you feel like crying please take a moment and gather yourself because the barbarians are at the gates and we'll need you to help fend them off."

"Yes, your highness. You can depend on me."

"I can tell that axe you're carrying is magical by the lightning bolts flickering across the blade," the king went on. "Make sure you bring that with you."

"Will do, your highness," Galen replied, "but I sure do wish Bronwyn were here. Just thinking of her brings a tear to my eye."

"I miss her too," said the king, "but I will also hold back my tears. We have a job to do."

We learned a lot about Galen, Bronwyn, and the king here, but it sure is stiff. Let's try it again with "business."

DIALOG TWO

"Bronwyn couldn't have survived the fire," Galen said.

"I know you loved her," the king replied, reaching out to put a hand on Galen's shoulder.

Galen turned away, wiping a tear from his eye with the back of his hand. He steadied himself on the windowsill and looked down upon the torches of the barbarian horde preparing for the coming day's siege.

"Gather yourself," the king commanded. "The kingdom will need you now."

Galen turned and looked at the king, but the monarch's eyes were on the axe in Galen's hand. The flickering blue lightning that traced the blade's edge reflected in a single tear that rolled down the king's cheek.

Galen tightened his grip on the axe handle, and the king said, "Bring that with you."

"I wish she were here to wield it," Galen said, then cleared his throat and stood up straight.

The king gave him a sad but respectful nod and said, "We have a job to do."

True, I used thirty more words in the second example, but we also know a little bit more about what's going on here.

Maybe the axe belonged to Bronwyn. We know that Galen and the king are in a tower. It's night because the barbarians have torches and are "preparing for the coming day's siege." I also used the actions of the characters—a hand on Galen's shoulder, his grip on the windowsill, the lightning reflecting in the king's tear—to convey an *emotional weight*. Someone saying "I'm sad" isn't going to conjure up that feeling.

Pacing Is Essential

When balancing big action and little action, find a good combination of pacing, movement, and environment. In the dialog example, the pacing of the action is slow. Galen turns, the king just stands there, and the barbarians aren't attacking yet. The movements the characters make convey a sense of claustrophobia, of impending trouble. The environment furthers that by placing them up above the action, though we (and they) know that soon they will have to descend into the hell of the barbarian attack.

But in big action set pieces, as when the steely eyed warriors are finally locked in mortal combat, blade-to-blade, *mano a mano*, we need to ask one very important question: WWJCD?

WHAT WOULD JACKIE CHAN DO?

If you've never seen a Jackie Chan movie, stop reading this right now, go rent at least two of them, watch them all the way through, then come back and start reading again.

Okay, now that you've seen at least two Jackie Chan movies, let's take a look at pacing, movement, and environment with this peculiar cinematic genius in mind.

Two warriors are locked in mortal combat—what would Jackie Chan do? He would make that sword fight fast and interesting. But how? There are an infinite number of ways, and that's why fantasy and science fiction will live forever. If you approach developing characters by asking questions, you can create action scenes by doing the same thing.

How many weapons do they have? What if there are two warriors, but only one weapon? Now one of them has to figure out how to avoid being stabbed while attempting to disarm his opponent and get the sword for himself. The combatants could trade this sword back and forth a number of times before one of them wins the day.

Where are they? They can use the environment to try to get the upper hand on each other. If they're in a room with furniture, how does that affect the fight? Can they hide behind something? Pick up a chair and throw it? What's the chair made of? Can the guy with the sword cut through it?

Are there other potential weapons? Is there a shield and crossed swords hanging on the wall? Are the swords rusty and dull, just old ornamental pieces, useless in a fight? Or can one of the fighters grab a sword? Is there a bottle of perfume on the dressing table? If one guy throws that in the other guy's face, will it blind him? Will it hinder them both, with the air so thick with perfume neither can take a deep breath?

The more you add to the environment of an action scene, the more tools you have to work with and the more varied and intense the fight becomes. Two guys fencing can be mildly interesting to some portion of your audience, but when one character is flipping through the rafters avoiding the sword blade while fashioning a makeshift bow out of clothes hangers and the princess's lingerie, it'll be interesting to everybody.

Keep Up to Speed

There can be more than one speed to the fight. One of the best movie action set pieces of all time is the giant bug scene in Peter Jackson's remake of *King Kong*. The pace—even the music throughout that scene—is torturously slow, and it's scary as hell. Our guy flipping through the rafters calls for fast pacing, but don't spare the slow and suspenseful moments, too.

The guy flipping through the rafters is moving (fast) in an interesting way (flipping) through an interesting part of the environment (the rafters—not a usual fencing arena), while using found items from his environment to tilt the balance by creating a makeshift weapon. Assuming you've established that the guy flipping through the rafters is unusually agile, and there's such a thing as elastic in this fantasy world, this scene is plausible, if not entirely realistic.

We've talked about this in several contexts: the sometimes subtle distinction between plausible and realistic. In a nutshell, *plausible* is when you shrug and think, "Okay, I can buy that."

In action scenes it's up to you to set your plausibility meter somewhere between wildly imaginative (logically impossible) and entirely in keeping with all natural and physical laws (backed up by well-documented evidence). If your writing is heavily shifted to the latter end of the scale, you're not writing fantasy anymore but maybe a really fascinating near-future science fiction police procedural. If it's too far off the other end, your book could be imaginative and weird, but it might be a stretch for even most fantasy readers to take seriously.

If you've established that your world contains magic shoes that allow people to walk on air, it's perfectly plausible that our combatants are outside, sliding across the wind, using clouds for cover while sneaking up on a foe who's flying on magical wings. Lots less realistic, but if you've set the rules for your world and adhere to them properly, no less plausible in context.

When it comes to approaching action scenes, author Mike Resnick advises, "Study the particular market . . . and put in a little more or a little less action than the competition—not so much or so little that it doesn't fit the format—to make [the] story stand out a bit."

WHAT'S AT STAKE?

This is the biggest question—the biggest series of questions—that any author should ask when developing an action scene. It goes back to the essential question of motivation. *Why* are these two guys trying to kill each other? What happens if Guy A wins? What happens if Guy B wins? What happens if neither win, but one manages to escape? If the guy flipping through the rafters is our hero, and he's in the princess's private bedchamber because he's gone ahead to make sure everything is safe—only to discover an assassin lying in wait for the princess—then the hero will have to find a way to kill the villain before the princess gets there. A clock is ticking, so things start going faster. What's at stake? The princess's life. Maybe the entire future of the realm.

"Have you ever read a lengthy action-packed scene, a fight, a chase, and even though it's full of *Sturm und Drang*, you're not very excited about it?" Kevin J. Anderson asks. "Probably because the action feels like filler, 'insert adventure here.'

"An action scene needs to emerge from the overall story," Anderson goes on. "If readers sense that this is just a placeholder (the pacing was slowing down, so the author just threw in a random encounter with a monster, they fight, they get away, the plot moves on), they don't feel it's important. You also have to know and care about the characters involved so you care who is being chased or threatened."

INTENSITY

What's the difference between action, violence, and gore?

- Action describes a scene in which there is a direct physical conflict over an important person, object, or ideal that's designed to resolve the conflict in a compelling way.

- Violence is a direct physical assault by one person or power on another for the purpose of intimidation, punishment, revenge, or some other one-sided motive.
- Gore is either of the first two without any motivation.

If Guy A and Guy B, flipping through the rafters of the princess's bedroom, are fighting because one wants to protect the princess while the other wants to harm her, that's action. If Guy B is an assassin, waiting in the bedroom for Guy A, whom he attacks and brutalizes, that's an act of violence. If Guy B is a homicidal maniac motivated by nothing other than the desire to kill people, and Guy A is a victim of convenience who just happened to wander by, that's gore.

With those definitions in mind, there can be action with blood and guts flowing, violence with no one being physically touched (the more subtle violence of intimidation and psychological abuse), and gore with no blood at all.

As a rule, most mainstream editors will tell you they aren't interested in gore, but that's because no one is interested in unmotivated violence. Finding a balance of blood and guts, action and violence, is part of what makes your writing your writing. Censor yourself if you're intentionally writing for a younger audience, or let the blood fly if you're willing to work on the edges of the genre. As in all things, balance will be rewarded.

CHAPTER 27
Everyone Needs a Little Romance

When some people hear (or read) the word *romance*, what springs to mind is the supermarket checkout aisle bodice-ripper. There are at least as many books on writing romance novels as there are on writing science fiction and fantasy novels, so if you have a passion for that genre, find a few of those for advice and inspiration. But beyond that, every genre of fiction can include romantic elements. In fact, it's rare for a book not to do so.

Heroes and villains alike are often motivated by love, or lust, or both. We've used these in examples throughout this book: the would-be priest who would rather go home and marry his small-town sweetheart, Guy A flipping around trying to use his girlfriend's undies as a weapon . . . Love and lust may be the most common motivators of human behavior. Those and money.

THE RULES APPLY TO ROMANCE
Both fantasy and science fiction require fully realized characters, and that usually includes some form of romance. People have done extraordinary things in the name of love, both positive and negative. When you're developing your characters, it's important to know whom they go home to every night—or whom they *hope* someday to go home to, or whom they *used* to go home to but can't anymore.

Like action and violence, a well-developed love interest is all about balance and motivation. Even the most male-dominated sword and sorcery or military science fiction story should still have some sexual dynamic.

One of the greatest fantasy stories of all time, "Red Nails" by Robert E. Howard, still might have had as much blade-swinging action with just Conan, but when Howard added Valeria to the mix, it burst into life. Conan loved her, and when her life was at stake, we were drawn into their story.

Here are some ways in which romance can enter your story.

ROMANTIC TRIANGLES AND OTHER SHAPES

Romantic triangles have been a common plot device for as long as people have been writing fiction. One man or woman is loved by two other men or women who compete for his or her affection. Romantic triangles in fiction have been further complicated by our society's increased openness to "alternative lifestyles." That triangle could be three men, three women, two men and one woman, or two women and one man. Who loves whom is entirely up to your imagination and what you're trying to say with your novel.

The classic romantic triangle can feel a little tired if you don't mix it up. One way to freshen things is by changing the shape. Who says confused lovers come in threes? Of course, the more people you add, the more complicated things get, and this could easily become confusing. Still, what about a romantic square that's two triangles joined together? Or three people competing for the affections of the same person? Fine, too.

SAME-SEX ROMANCE

In all honesty, the science fiction and fantasy genres can have a conservatism all their own, and it's a rare thing to find a mainstream genre novel that overtly stretches the boundaries in terms of sex, but there certainly is no rule to say that any number or variety of fantasy characters can't be lesbian, gay, bisexual, or transgender. And fantasy and science fiction, with the introduction of magical or high-tech elements, can give whole new options to exploring alternative sexualities no one but you has ever dreamed of.

EROTICISM

As was true with action, the intensity you give to your sex scenes is a question of balance. There's a strong market for erotic fantasy that moves very close to the edge of pornography. But don't go past your personal comfort zone and try to force out blow-by-blow sex scenes (no pun intended). If you're a fan of erotic fantasy, go for it. If you aren't, don't.

You should put as much thought and effort into crafting creative sex scenes as you put into writing creative action scenes, though you won't be asking so much what Jackie Chan would do as what Jenna Jameson would do. I could get in trouble demanding that you rent two of her videos, so let's go ahead and call that optional for consenting adults.

CHAPTER 28

USE HUMOR WITH CARE

On his deathbed, the British actor and theatrical director Sir Donald Wolfit reportedly said, "Dying is easy, comedy is hard." Though he was talking about acting, his words hold just as true for writers across every medium. Comedy has a place in fantasy, to be sure, but you will need to proceed with the utmost caution. Wolfit wasn't kidding. Comedy is *hard*.

In Chapter 12, we mentioned the supporting character who provides comic relief. A big percentage of mainstream fantasy and science fiction novels include a character who knows when to ease the tension with a quick-witted one-liner, or to temper the earnest pseudo-political or quasi-religious rhetoric with a handy moment of slapstick.

If you're not a funny person in real life—if you don't routinely and spontaneously make the people around you laugh—don't try it in your writing. Better your book remains serious and moody, devoid of humor, than sprinkled with clunkers.

While I was editing Paul Kidd's Forgotten Realms novel *Council of Blades*, he was in England writing for Monty Python alum Eric Idle. *Council of Blades* is a hoot—but the Realms fans hated it.

This was a lesson Paul and I learned: You have to be careful and even-handed with comedic fantasy and science fiction lest fans think you're making fun of the genre, and by association, making fun of *them*. Genre readers can embrace you like one of their own, sustaining careers that last decades, or they can drop you like a load of bricks. If they feel they're being mocked, good luck ever selling them another book.

I am a fan of fantasy and science fiction. I happily identify myself as a geek, a nerd, a Trekkie, a gamer . . . I've made fantasy novels and *Dungeons & Dragons* not only my hobby but also my career. I take it very seriously, and when someone comes along and smugly dismisses the genre, I can't help but feel they've smugly dismissed me. And I don't number among my friends people who have no respect for me.

Have respect for the genre, and your readers. Be certain your lighter moments invite your readers to laugh with you, rather than make them think you're laughing at them.

To Sum Up

The little things that people do while talking to each other, which we'll call "business," can lend a depth to a scene that's otherwise just meant to get some information across. Let a nod sometimes replace a spoken "yes," a tear tell us someone is upset, or a fist pounded on a tabletop convey anger.

For bigger action set pieces, look to the movies for inspiration. But regardless of the size and scope of your action, remember that it has to be strongly motivated. If there's nothing at stake, there's no reason for the fight.

These definitions bear repeating:

- Action describes a direct physical conflict over an important person, object, or ideal that's designed to resolve the conflict in a compelling and exciting way.
- Violence is a direct physical assault by one person or power over another for the purpose of intimidation, punishment, revenge, or other one-sided motives.
- Gore is either of the first two without any motivation.

The level of intensity of action and violence is up to you, but there should never be any unmotivated action or violence (gore) in your book. Ever.

Every novel should have romantic elements. Characters are often strongly motivated by love. As with action and violence, the intensity of erotic scenes is all about your comfort level. Humor should be used with utmost care—only if you're funny and only in a way that shows proper respect for the genre and its readership.

STEP SIX | FINISHING TOUCHES

"Novels start with a feeling of something in my brain that cannot be explained."

—J. M. McDERMOTT, author of *Last Dragon*

It may seem as though we're almost done. *We* are, but *you're* only just beginning. Now that you've got a good sense of what story you're going to write, which characters will populate it, what those characters are after, and which world they'll live in, you have only one more thing to do.

You have to actually write the thing.

This section will offer advice on how to get writing and keep writing, while keeping a firm hand on all your notes and conceptual stuff. This is the part most people don't necessarily think of, but it can make or break a novel.

CHAPTER 29

KEEP IT FRESH

I'll assume you are not already a *New York Times* bestselling author of an ongoing series of popular fantasy or science fiction novels. You have not already carved out your corner of the genre and defined a world to call your own. That being the case, you'll need your book to show, really from the very first paragraph, that though you haven't yet, you're ready, willing, and able to do just that.

"From the publishing perspective, like all genres, fantasy is utterly trend-driven," author and critic Paul Witcover says. I think he's right, but unfortunately new authors are often under undue pressure to establish the *next* trend. If you follow too close in the footsteps of the last bestselling author, you run the risk of appearing to have cobbled together some kind of knock-off. Then you have to hope to find a publisher looking to knock off the last bestseller. It can happen, but it'll leave you with some baggage that might be hard to dump later in your career.

In fact, new authors are under a bit *more* pressure to be original than established authors. After all, if a publisher is going to invest thousands of dollars in your book, and you have no track record, you're going to have to give them something special.

"The trick," advises Paul Park, "is to make [fantasy worlds] familiar enough to evoke and resonate with an entire tradition, while unfamiliar enough to resist melting into other, more primary texts. An accumulation of specific detail is how you accomplish this, and while there might be limits on what you can cram into the actual story, there are no limits on what it would behoove you to imagine."

LOOK TO THE ARCHETYPES

Genre readers expect a certain percentage of archetypes in any book they read, regardless of the author. With established authors they tend to look for that author's tropes—his richly realized future Earth, her erotic fairyland—but if no one but you and your close friends know your work, you'll have to think a little bit about what makes your book "fantasy" or "science fiction" while at the same time keeping it original.

Certain key components, like elves in fantasy or robots in science fiction, are free for the taking. No one, even the estates of J. R. R. Tolkien or Isaac Asimov, can sue you for picking those archetypes up and running with them. But if you don't give them a unique spin, agents and editors will shrug you off.

If the robot is an archetype, what makes your robot different than Asimov's, Lucas's, or anyone else's? C-3PO's gold "skin" was reminiscent of the Maria robot in Fritz Lang's *Metropolis*, but C-3PO's personality couldn't be any more different. Lucas gave a nod back to one of the first science fiction movie epics, but he created robots all his own, robots that have stood the test of time. If you take any advice in this book, remember this:

Use every archetype in the genre toolbox, but make them your own.

What unique twists can you put on a robot or an elf? Appeal to all five senses. C-3PO has a distinctive voice, for instance. Elves usually have pointed ears, but do they have to? Could they have unusual eyes? Could your elves have inherent magical powers that no other author has ascribed to them? Ask questions. The most difficult hurdle any new writer has to cross is the line between original and derivative.

"Good Artists Borrow, Great Artists Steal"

This quote has been attributed to Pablo Picasso, but he probably stole it from someone else. Whoever said it second was right, and though the quote is open to interpretation, let's think about what it means for our purposes.

If your robot is C-3PO with silver "skin" instead of gold, you've borrowed George Lucas's robot for your book. If your robot is C-3PO but he's not in the shape of a human, he lacks the English accent, and instead of being jittery and frightened all the time he's kind of a douche, then you've stolen it, and you are on your way to being a great artist.

Exactly Alike but Completely Different

But, you might be asking, if I change all that about C-3PO, he isn't C-3PO anymore. Exactly, but then in what way will it still be like C-3PO?

I'm assuming you started with C-3PO for a reason. In Star Wars, he's the robot who translates for the hero, cautions the hero not to act so impulsively, provides a little comic relief, and gets himself into tight spots that force the hero to rescue him. Your robot could fill similar roles in your story, but he's also a unique robotic creation all your own. Always bring your own fresh ideas, even to the old archetypes.

I wish I could tell you that's easier than you think, but I'm going to have to side with Pyr editorial director Lou Anders, who says a first-time author has to "be better than brilliant." He explains, "There are so so so so many fantasy manuscripts doing the rounds out there. And the problem isn't that it's all drek. It's that it's all average, competent, but not exuberantly good. Your writing needs to make an editor leap up out of his/her chair. Good writing outs."

CHAPTER 30

Avoid Anachronisms

Anachronisms are the most common and most insidious disease of science fiction and fantasy. They can take many forms, popping up at all the least convenient times, and sometimes leaving authors and editors scratching their heads over how to fix ones they've found or how to apologize for ones discovered by readers. You'd better know what an anachronism is, learn how to spot them, and spend a good portion of your writing time cleaning them up.

An anachronism is an unintentional mistake in chronology.

Here are two fun examples:

The space shuttle Dr. Floyd takes to the space station in *2001: A Space Odyssey* is operated by Pan Am, an airline that went out of business in 1991.

Stephen King's *The Green Mile* is set in the fictional Cold Mountain Penitentiary in Louisiana in 1932, and prominently features death row inmates executed by means of the electric chair. But the electric chair wasn't used in Louisiana until 1941.

ANACHRONISMS IN SCIENCE FICTION

In the example from *2001*, we see the bane of the science fiction author's existence: Your story is overtaken by events. Who could know in 1968 when that movie was made that one of the biggest airlines in the world would be out of business in less than thirty years? The movie was set in 2001 and included commercial flights to one of at least two moon cities. The story included an artificially intelligent (and homicidal) computer with full voice recognition, but Dr. Floyd had to spend money on a video phone booth—I guess you couldn't get cell service in orbit. The story also made reference to a manned mission to Jupiter that left Earth in 2002? Where have I been?

This movie was written and conceived by Arthur C. Clarke and Stanley Kubrick, two shockingly intelligent men who made extensive use of technical advisors from NASA and various space program contractors. They worked under what turned out to be the mistaken assumption that our government would continue to fund the manned space program at Apollo levels for the next thirty-five years. Oh, if only that had been the case.

How do you avoid these kinds of errors? Some authors refuse to get specific about the date, or they get specific about the fact that there is no date: *A long time ago, in a galaxy far, far away.* Others, like Frank Herbert, go so far into the future we're ready to accept anything. *Dune* is set in the year 21,000 AD, or somewhere around there. Then there's *1984*, a novel that George Orwell certainly didn't intend as an accurate view of the future. Orwell was writing about the world he saw around him in the 1940s: the post-war adoption of fascist principles and the establishment of the totalitarian oligarchy, which was overtly manifested in Russia, but rather more subtle in Orwell's native Britain and here in the United States. It's actually surprising how much Orwell got right in terms of the prosecution of the Cold War, which shifted from the Soviet Union (Eurasia) to Radical Islam (Eastasia) without most of us batting an eye, and Newspeak is a handier moniker than "political correctness," isn't it? Scary, actually. Orwell also sort of gets around the problem right at the beginning of the novel when Winston Smith says he's not entirely sure it *is* 1984, since time-keeping has become frighteningly slippery in the world of Oceania.

The best near-future science fiction follows in Orwell's footsteps. Science fiction really has always been more about our world today than it is about any attempt to do the impossible: accurately predict the future.

Consider the risks of anachronisms in science fiction with great caution. Despite great care, you may be stuck with *Star Trek*'s Ensign Chekov musing about life in Leningrad something like two hundred years after the Russians changed the name back to St. Petersburg. In other words, the future will catch up to you. But if your characters, your writing, and your message are enduring, you'll get the same pass that Clarke and Kubrick have gotten, and that Orwell got. We'll have to wait until 21,001 AD or so to see how well *Dune* stood up.

GETTING IT WRONG IN FANTASY

In fantasy, though, avoiding anachronism can be harder. Lots harder.

Historical fantasy is *really* hard. Say you want to write a fantasy novel set in the Roman Empire. You imagine what it would have been like if the Roman legions employed cavalry mounted on flying dragons. You need to submerge yourself in that historical period. You need to be obsessive about it. Could a character be wearing glasses? Would he have ever eaten an orange? Broccoli? Tomatoes? How did the Romans treat wounds or sicknesses? If you don't know, never assume. Check your own facts before an angry reader checks them for you.

Other forms of fantasy pose fewer—but different—risks of anachronisms. After all, if your world is entirely divorced from Earth and any of its cultures, you are in complete control of things like food and medicine and so on. You could have your medieval fantasy people doing CPR if you want. Why not? They can wear glasses, wristwatches, or even shoot each other with guns. But refer back to the chapter on technology and use elements like these with great care. If you envision a steampunk world, then all the technological gloves are off. A steam-powered cell phone? Okay. But if you're committing to a medieval level of technology, go forth and learn what its limits are.

CHAPTER 31

FOLLOW YOUR OWN RULES

It's your story. You are in charge of how magic works, how your faster-than-light starship flies, whether or not robots can cry, and the subtle differences between a red elf and a purple elf.

But . . .

Once you've set that rule, it must not change unless you make it a part of your story that something has changed.

Remember, don't just tell us; show us. If there's no reason for the change, if it doesn't move your story forward, don't do it. Leave the magic, the starship, the robots, and the elves the same on page 200 as they were on page one.

Consistency leads to plausibility, which, more than anything else, determines the success of your story—and I don't mean the financial success of your book, but whether or not your story works as a story. Truth be told, the financial success won't likely happen if you ignore your own rules, either.

KEEP NOTES

The first thing you *must* do, no matter what, is keep notes. And no, mental notes are not good enough, even if you're sure you have a photographic memory. But where? How?

Here's some good advice from J. M. McDermott: "Excel spreadsheets are a marvelous way of collating vast seas of notes and information. You can build whole 'books' of spreadsheet data to quickly sift through your world and your notes, and keep it open in the background while you write. Simply 'Alt-Tab' over, and check or update your notes and 'Alt-Tab' back. You never even take your hands off the keyboard."

But you say you don't want to learn Excel? Okay, use a Word file. Alternately, Mac has a Stickies function that could work for small batches of notes for short stories. Or you can always buy a blank notebook from your local dollar store, office supply shop, or pharmacy. Write in that notebook using pencil stubs, cheap ballpoints, or gold fountain pens—whatever's handy.

Avoid Rituals at All Costs

Rituals are excuses for avoiding work and creativity. If you think you can only write your notes in that lovely leather-bound notebook your boyfriend gave you and only when it's dark and only when it's raining, you're fooling yourself. Write anywhere, at any time.

What form should those notes take? You tell me. Some people are very systematic in their note taking while others scribble down bits of disconnected information and gather them later. You need to figure this out for yourself, because different people have different thought processes. Keep in mind that no one but you need ever read these notes, so don't get hung up on finesse.

KEEP A WORD LIST

The word list is an indispensable tool in writing fantasy and science fiction, so set aside a separate file on your computer or set of pages in your notebook for this.

Obviously there's no need to make a list of every word in your novel, but you should list every word you invent, including character and place names. This is your primary tool to make sure that *Bronwyn* doesn't turn into *Bronwin* then into *Bonwyyn* as you go along. Don't be surprised if your editor asks you for this list at some point. It will help a copy editor fix mistakes for you before you make a fool of yourself in print. Arrange these words alphabetically—Word can do that for you.

ADD WORDS TO THE SPELL-CHECK FUNCTION

If you're writing on a computer, you need to use your computer's spell-check function. No, it's not cheating; it's a useful tool. Be careful about believing everything it tells you, though. If it tries to fix something you're sure is right, don't automatically believe it, but also don't automatically reject it—use it as a kind of alert system. If it calls something out, you know you have to double-check it.

Spell-checkers get mighty confused by fantasy and science fiction. Your strange invented names for things won't be in your software's dictionary, but the program will give you an opportunity to add that word to a custom dictionary. When your spell-checker doesn't recognize *Bronwyn*, go back to your word list and make sure that's the spelling you intended. If it is, add *Bronwyn* to your custom dictionary. Then, if you inadvertently switch to *Bronwin* later on, your computer will point that out to you and give you the option of changing all occurrences of *Bronwin* back to *Bronwyn*.

On the other hand, if the dictionary automatically recognizes the name, maybe it isn't as original as you thought it was. Is that okay? Should you check with what that name means, in what other books a character named *Bronwyn* might have appeared? Do you want to rethink that name?

If you're *not* writing on a computer, take a moment to get a hold of yourself. Then go buy one and learn how to use it. It has been an essential piece of equipment for professional writers for more than twenty years. Yes, you too.

DRAW PICTURES

Many authors doodle while they work, drawing maps, diagrams, and seemingly meaningless squiggles. If you think visually and want to sketch what your starship looks like, or having a floor plan of the castle helps you visualize a complicated chase through the dungeons, by all means draw. Again, don't suffer from Over-Presentation Syndrome. No one will ever see these doodles, maps, and diagrams—no one in public anyway, though your editor might like to be able to hand your drawings and notes off to a professional artist to draw a map for your book.

YOUR WORK BIBLE

Eventually this notebook, Word, or Excel file will end up being what writers refer to as a "bible." It's a book you refer to for wisdom and guidance, in this case on the specific subject of your imagined world and the characters who inhabit it.

According to author Kevin J. Anderson, his "most important step in creating a new world for a series is to develop and write the bible. I write entries on the major cities (or worlds), the races, the history, the politics, the religion, the society, the economy, and other specific things to the book. As I write the biographies of the characters, I learn how they interconnect. As I develop the history, I get ideas for legends, conflicts, and then I need more characters to flesh that out, to pick up interesting professions I have created in earlier versions of the bible. The creative process spirals out from there, and *I keep asking questions* [emphasis added]. Along the way, I will do the specific research I need, which might also lead to additional ideas, to be included in the next iteration of the expanding bible."

Once this bible is all done—a great notebook full of lists and doodles and so on—you have a rulebook: a set of laws for how your world works, who your characters are, and how things interrelate. Does that mean that once that bible is written it should be considered holy and inviolate, never in any way reinterpreted or questioned?

Of course not.

After all, no one but you is ever going to read this bible. If a particular idea you were sure was pure gold three months ago is sitting in your notes like Hoover Dam, holding back that really great idea you had this morning, think through how it affects what you've written already and what you plan to have happen next, then go ahead and change the rule. Your notes are not meant to *confine* you, they're meant to *inform* you.

Now follow the new rule to the letter, right up until the precise moment you decide to revise that rule—which is different from breaking it—in a really fascinating way that will make your story a million times better. Then write down the revised rule and how and why it's different from the old rule—remember the power crystal that makes the purple fire spell bigger?

That's what I mean.

TO SUM UP

An author of science fiction and fantasy needs to *read* science fiction and fantasy. You should be familiar with the archetypes of the genres, and conversant in their primary texts. Then you need to consciously construct your work as a fresh take on those accepted tropes. If you're unpublished and unknown, you have to be prepared to be held to a high standard of originality. Follow trends at your own risk, and if you're smart and creative enough, set them.

As you're reading through your own work, keep a sharp eye out for anachronisms. Be careful setting the precise date for your science fiction story unless you have a very specific point to make. Star Wars might eventually appear dated as special effects get better and better, but it will never be "wrong," because only George Lucas knows what really happened a long time ago, in a galaxy far, far away.

But even Lucas gets in trouble when he fails to follow both the rules he's set for himself (like the sudden, inexplicable introduction of micro-organisms to explain the Force), or rules of common usage (the word *parsec*, which is a unit of distance, apparently used to indicate speed).

Take detailed notes, organized as best you can, and make use of every tool at your disposal—from spreadsheets to spell-checkers—to make sure that you don't sacrifice plausibility just by being carelessly inconsistent. Plausibility fuels the suspension of disbelief that fantasy and science fiction readers want to bring into the experience of reading your novel. Help them like you—stick to the rules you've set for your world.

PART III
THE BUSINESS

"I think there are all sorts of ways to break into the business and be successful at it. If you are willing to put in the time and effort, study on the craft, read everything you can get your hands on, and be patient, you will find a way."

—TERRY BROOKS, author of *The Sword of Shannara*

There is a long list of books out there that will tell you all about the book business, and most of them are reasonably accurate, even the ones that make it seem as though "breaking in" is either surprisingly easy or impossibly hard. It's actually somewhere in the middle . . . surprisingly hard. The "surprisingly" stems from all the reasons your manuscript is rejected that you couldn't possibly have thought of. Sometimes you just catch an editor or agent on a bad day.

I know, now you're cringing, getting righteously angry with me that I'm about to abdicate all responsibility for you, your book, and your career, after getting you to pay me to help you. I understand, and though I can't tell you that the publishing business is all sunshine and ponies and happy rainbows, I can tell you that it's possible to get published. I did it, and so did all of the friends who've added their wisdom to these proceedings and whom I've worked with in some cases for more than a decade.

I have been in the happiest position any editor can be in: I've accepted authors' first novels.

At the same time, I've also rejected probably a thousand manuscripts for every one that got through. But don't lose heart. Those are better odds than the lottery, especially since *there are ways to increase your odds!*

Read on.

CHAPTER 32

GET PUBLISHED

In John D. Leonard's 1958 *Harvard Crimson* article "Cocktails with Truman Capote," Capote claimed that he had never received a rejection letter. If this is true, then he's the only one. Every other author has, at one time or another, gotten something along these lines from an editor (or an editor's assistant, or an intern):

> Thank you for considering GIGANTIC PUBLISHING CONGLOMERATE, INC. as a possible publisher for your novel (or cookbook, or memoir, or telephone directory), but we regret that we are unable to publish your work at this time and wish you the best of luck with your future endeavors.

Truth be told, they probably don't even really wish you luck. More likely they wish you would just go away. If you do just go away, they will not miss you. If you try again, chances are you'll get exactly the same response—and I mean *exactly*. But with practice and persistence, eventually you may receive a very different kind of letter. I did. And so did Terry Brooks, and thousands of other authors.

THE MAGIC OF THE BREAKTHROUGH

Everybody "gets in" in a different way, at a different time, with a different book, for different reasons. Pyr editor Lou Anders advises aspiring authors to "join and participate in the SF&F community. Not only is there a great deal of learning by osmosis to be done, but you will already be part of the industry you are looking to become part of. All business endeavors benefit from relationships. Publishing is no different. This does not mean that if you buy an editor a beer he/she will buy your manuscript! But that if you want to learn about the business you are trying to break into, going to where that business is conducted might be a wise move."

The areas most open to unpublished authors are conventions. Not everyone can afford to fly to one of the major conventions, but almost every large city has some kind of a science fiction or comic book convention. Start local, and get yourself to the biggest convention you can afford to get to. While stopping short of being creepy and stalkery, introduce yourself to professionals there. Go to seminars rather than spending your days in the anime room. Listen to the stories and advice from seminar panels—contradictory as it will be. Absorb all of it and accept that your entrance into publishing will combine some elements of other authors' success stories with a unique twist you'll be able to call your own.

GET YOURSELF AN AGENT

Agents are as important to the publishing process now as they ever were, maybe more so. Just ignore the myth that says that no editor will read your work unless it comes from an agent and no agent will read your work unless you already have at least one book published. If this were the case, then once everyone who's currently writing novels dies, there will be no more novels.

In fact, new authors are breaking in all the time. Some editors won't read unagented submissions, but most agents I know will read unsolicited manuscripts, and if they find something they think they can sell, they will sign you on as at least a "hip pocket" client. That means the agent likes this one book and will try to sell it but is cautious about committing to your career until there's some traction on that first manuscript.

For the majority of aspiring authors, it's better to be a hip pocket client than not to be a client at all, so don't be too wary of this kind of arrangement. Having someone who has at least that much confidence in your work is a major first step. According to author J. M. McDermott, "Writers tend to know less about writing, in general, than agents and editors. Writers tend to only work with one type of writer: themselves."

Sample Query Letter

Ethan Ellenberg was kind enough to write a sample query letter for us. Don't copy this word for word (especially if you plan to send it to Ethan), but look to it for inspiration and instruction. Notice how simple it is. He spent exactly forty-five words on what the book is actually about—twenty more than a Hollywood log line. The next sentence after that pimps the thing a little bit. Don't be afraid to sell yourself and your book. If you can't get excited about it, why should anyone else? But be careful: "This is the finest fantasy novel ever written and will forever revolutionize this tired old genre" is not going to win you points. It's going to make you look like a jackass.

SAMPLE QUERY LETTER

Dear Ethan,

I'm enclosing the first three chapters and the synopsis for my completed fantasy novel, ETERNAIA.

ETERNAIA is the story of a small group of bored aristocrats who realize the world they are in is synthetic and though they neither age nor get sick they desperately plot to escape their world back to the world of sickness and death—real life. I've created compelling characters and a fascinating new world that harbors lots of secrets and surprises certain to hook even the most jaded fan of the genre.

As soon as you express interest in the sample material, I'd be happy to forward you the balance of the book.

Sincerely,
Ms. or Mr. Brand New Writer

In query letters like this, comparing your work to successful books is a time-honored tradition, but it's a little risky. Be realistic about the books you're comparing yourself to—realistic and *positive*. "It's like The Lord of the Rings but less boring, mixed with a much better written *Twilight*" sends you back into jackass territory. "It's *Mein Kampf* meets the Bible" might get you on some kind of FBI watch list, but not an agent's client list. "Combines the innocence of Harry Potter and the nonstop action of *HALO*" might get you somewhere.

This letter would work as well to send to editors who are open to unsolicited, unagented submissions. *Unsolicited* means the editor didn't ask you for it; you're sending it in blind, hoping it'll be read and loved. Publishers, especially those who let the word get out that they'll read unsolicited manuscripts, get a lot of them. How many? Hundreds.

A few hundred every year? That doesn't sound like so much. No—hundreds *a day* in some cases.

If your query letter strikes a chord with that agent or editor, he or she might ask to see some or all of your manuscript. Hopefully you've actually written the book and can respond right away. But keep in mind that just because someone has asked to read it, you still have a ways to go before a decision is made to publish it. The book still has to be good.

When an agent or editor picks up your manuscript or query letter, you have only a few minutes—maybe even seconds—to make your case. You need to accomplish two things in that first minute or so:

1. Come off as a sane, balanced professional. Be sure to use only white paper. Fancy colors or expensive paper will make you look less professional: a rookie trying to impress with everything except what needs to be impressive—your writing.
2. Show that you're expending your energy on your story, not on some goofy gimmick. Chances are high that no one wants to read a book that is half written in Ancient Greek. The same for a pop-up book aimed at adults. These are expensive to manufacture, so even a good one for kids has to be *awesome* before a publisher will invest that heavily in its success. And if your book is meant to be read in two directions at the same time, like Mark Z. Danielewski's *Only Revolutions*, well then like Danielewski you better have already been successful with a book as extraordinary as *House of Leaves* or that's an almost certain pass.

Do not ever tell people that you know you're "the next [insert name of popular author here]" and for the love of all that's holy, never ever take potshots at any other author. Telling an agent "I can write circles around [bestselling author who unbeknownst to you just had dinner at the agent's apartment last night]" is not going to make that come true.

Keep it professional: simple, to the point, realistic, and positive. Any other brilliant idea is a bad idea. Yes, even that one. Just don't.

Stay Humble

Literary manager and film and television producer Brendan Deneen cautions authors to avoid arrogance. "Self-confidence is a great trait but certain 'new' authors act as if they're already bestselling authors with the attitude to match. A dose of humility and a lot of good humor goes a long, long way in this industry."

All this presupposes that you have a completed manuscript in hand. Do not try to sell a novel you haven't written yet. If you have a great idea, hurray for you. So does everyone. No one gives a rat's ass about your great idea unless you are an established author with several bestsellers behind you. For now, if you've actually written the book, it's an original work that is yours to sell, and the story and characters are compelling, the prose sparkling, there is a market out there for it.

Finding the Right Agent

Where do you find agents and editors willing to read unsolicited manuscripts? There are a number of online sources just a keyword search away. The Internet has made getting this information faster, easier, and a little bit more reliable. But exercise caution. If the website you find was last updated in 2006, ignore everything on it and move on. In this business, 2006 might as well be 206. Out of date information isn't any help.

Confirm that the editor or agent is still with the company. If you send your manuscript to someone who was fired six months ago, the editors who remain are likely to ignore you—you obviously weren't professional enough to do your research. Give them a handy excuse to toss out an unsolicited submission and they'll happily take it.

Never, ever *call* or even e-mail an editor or agent to pitch anything or follow up on an unsolicited submission. This is both completely unprofessional and an intrusion on the editor or agent's time. If you—and the thousands of authors like you—grind the editors and agents to a halt, *no one* will get published.

Waiting sucks, but it's part of the publishing process. Rejection sucks, but it's part of it, too. If you are really serious about being a published author, this is the world you've entered, and this is part of how it has always worked. Be patient, assume you'll be rejected at least once, and keep at it. "Luck is a big part of this business," Terry Brooks cautions, "but as Kevin Anderson is fond of saying, 'The harder I work, the luckier I get.' "

Mike Resnick maintains that "selling the fourth book is always more difficult than selling the first. You sell your first on promise; you sell your fourth on your track record, and your publisher probably hasn't poured any promotional money into your first few." This is a tough business, and every year it gets a little less forgiving.

Critic and author Paul Witcover offers this simple advice: "Above all, keep writing, keep submitting, keep revising."

Remember, you might be rejected a thousand times, but it only takes one "yes" to launch a career.

CHAPTER 33

DO IT FOR A LIVING

In a letter to H. P. Lovecraft, Robert E. Howard wrote:

> I could have studied law, or gone into some other occupation, but none offered me the freedom writing did—and my passion for freedom is almost an obsession . . . Personal liberty may be a phantom, but I hardly think anybody would deny that there is more freedom in writing than there is in slaving in an iron foundry, or working—as I have worked—from twelve to fourteen hours, seven days a week, behind a soda fountain. I have worked as much as eighteen hours a day at my typewriter, but it was work of my own choosing . . . I've always had a honing to make my living by writing, ever since I can remember, and while I haven't been a howling success in that line, at least I've managed for several years now to get by without grinding at some time clock-punching job.

Is this your dream? To be a full-time writer, banging away at the keyboard entirely at your leisure, writing nothing but what most inspires you, and being paid millions of dollars a year in the process, achieving fame and glory?

If you want to write a science fiction or fantasy novel in order to get rich, stop now. Chances are, you will not be paid at all, let alone get "rich," at least by most people's standards. In this genre, there are a small number of very successful authors, a few who could be described as millionaires. But the overwhelming majority of the authors I work with hold down a full-time "day job" in one industry or another. There are a number of teachers, at least one lawyer, and a bunch of people who are editors or otherwise involved in the publishing or entertainment business.

DON'T WRITE TO GET RICH

Writing is a terrible way to try to make a living. Even if you're fairly successful, money comes to you in clumps, and it's unreliable. A lot of what may affect your income is out of your control.

When I think about the subject of authors and money, I'm reminded of a line from *Citizen Kane*: "It's no trick, making a lot of money, if all you want is to make a lot of money."

If you want to be rich in a hurry, sell insurance. If you want to be *really* rich and have a few years to achieve it, invent a sustainable clean energy source. But as far as being a novelist is concerned, you'll find that money comes slowly, rarely, and in small doses.

Which reminds me of another line from a movie, this one called *Orange County.* A teenager appeals to his wealthy but absentee father for money to go to an Ivy League university to study under his favorite novelist. His father rejects the idea on the basis that there's no money in being a writer. When the son mentions Stephen King, Anne Rice, and Tom Clancy, the father replies, "That's three people! *In the history of literature!*"

You know who wrote those lines? A writer.

Do this for everything *but* the money. Only if you're writing for the love of the game will you ever end up with a book that people respond to, and pay for.

If You Want to Be a Writer, Write

On the subject of work habits I'll refer you to my blog for an entry entitled "Save the Bullshit Excuses," but here's one that's important to pass on to you now. Many books and articles on writing advise something like this: Find a safe place to write—an office, a nook, some kind of cave in which you can work in absolute silence and solitude, surrounded by inspirational knickknacks or whatever.

It seems like good advice, and for years I followed it and wrote very little.

Never do this. Buy a laptop as soon as you possibly can. Write while sitting on the living room couch, in bed, at a coffee house or bar, at the library, on the bus or plane or train—write everywhere and whenever. If you find yourself thinking, "Well, I can't write without, unless, or until . . ." then stop right there, get your laptop fired up, and write something. I don't even care what it is, just write.

Write when the kids are asleep or running around you in circles screaming at the top of their lungs, with the television on or off, with or without music, where people are talking or silent. Do not ever let yourself be limited to a place, a time, or a set of circumstances in which you can write. Free yourself, and your words will follow.

If you have a deadline, consider yourself lucky. If someone cares enough about what you're writing to want it at a certain time, honor that. Would you blow deadlines at your "day job"? Would you fail to pick up your kids from school? Would you pay your taxes on April 16? No? Then why would you keep your editor waiting?

MAINTAIN RELATIONSHIPS

At the other side of that deadline is your agent, your editor, or both. "I think a writer's relationship with an editor is crucial," Terry Brooks explains. "I've had three: Lester del Rey, Owen Lock, and Betsy Mitchell. All have taught me something, all have been committed to making my work better, all have been friends. I don't think I could function if that wasn't so. The writer/editor relationship is not all that different from a marriage. There needs to be understanding, give and take, and deep respect."

The Editor Is There to Help

Remember that your editor is there to help you make your book the best book it can be. Take any constructive criticism from your editor very seriously. This is the time to address concerns, not after the book hits the shelves.

THE IMPORTANCE OF THE AGENT

Agents can be very helpful, but it pays to be wary. A minority of people who call themselves agents are either bad at it or are engaging in fraud. Organizations like the Association of Authors' Representatives can help you weed out the bad ones.

Warning signs of a bad or an unscrupulous agent include:

- The agent charges you "reading fees." The *only* fee an agent should charge is a commission (usually between 10 percent and 20 percent of the advance and royalty they negotiate on your behalf).
- The agent tries to sell you "editorial services," for which you will be charged. This falls outside the function of the agent. The agent should help you with your proposal, but it's the editor's job to help you with the manuscript.
- The agent sends out your manuscript to a large list of editors and publishers without bothering to find out if they accept this sort of material. If your agent can't tell you who he's sent your work to and why—if the agent can't articulate a clear plan for getting your manuscript into the right hands—that's a bad sign.

Salespeople Versus Lawyers

Agents come in two flavors: salespeople and lawyers. You want the former. (If you need a separate lawyer, get a separate lawyer.) Agents should be, like salespeople, knowledgeable and enthusiastic champions of your work, who know where the customers (the editors) are and know how to negotiate and close a deal. At the same time, agents should nurture and maintain their (and your) relationship with the editor and the publishing house. If an agent complains to you about the staff at a publishing company, that is *not* a good agent.

Editors should never recommend agents. Don't ask them to.

Think of it this way: What if I was an ethically challenged editor who wanted to get your book for as little money as I could get away with? If you come represented by an agent I know is going to fight for you, I call you personally and tell you your agent is a big jerk and you have to get a "better" one, and I just happen to have a friend who I think would be perfect for you. But actually my "friend" is an agent I have some kind of under-the-table sweetheart deal with or who I know is easy to roll over for whatever crap offer I throw his way. Then we all pretend you've been taken care of when in fact you've been defrauded.

Because I don't do that sort of thing, and don't want anyone to think I do, as an editor I won't recommend a particular agent, and I won't warn you away from a particular agent. If you have an agent I think is a jerk, I'll still do my best to get your book, but I have corporate masters the same as any other editor and can't just spend money willy-nilly, or change the corporation's accounts payable system on one agent's whim. So if you have an agent who fights for the wrong stuff and lets a good deal fall through, I'm disappointed, you're disappointed, and I can't really ever tell you why.

CHAPTER 34
EMBRACE THE TIE-IN

Surely there is no form of published writing that is as misunderstood, by both its fans and detractors, as tie-in fiction. It's constantly dismissed in the science fiction and fantasy community as bad writing. So-called "mainstream" authors make insulting presumptions, accusing tie-in authors of being glorified fan-fiction writers. On the other end of the spectrum are die-hard fans who take it a bit too seriously, climbing into the text in search of the tiniest mistake in continuity.

Tie-in fiction (also known as *shared world, game-related, media-related,* etc.) is a story set in a world or universe of someone else's creation. Most commonly the world was created first for a game, a movie, a television series, or a comic book series. There are huge lines of novels based on games like *Dungeons & Dragons*, *Warhammer* and *Warhammer 40,000*, and *World of Warcraft*; movies like Star Wars and *Terminator;* TV series like *Star Trek, Buffy the Vampire Slayer,* or *Doctor Who*; and a wealth of comic book superheroes. Some of these novels are novelizations, while others are tie-ins—more on the distinction to follow.

WORK-FOR-HIRE
Both tie-ins and novelizations are done on a work-for-hire basis. That means that the source of the novel—from a basic sketch of the world all the way down to a fully realized outline—is provided by the publisher or licensor (an entity, usually a corporation, that owns the property in question; for instance, Lucasfilm owns Star Wars

and Wizards of the Coast owns Dragonlance). The author is hired to complete that novel.

In many cases, the publisher or licensor is open to ideas from the author, and authors often enjoy wide latitude in creating new characters and inventing their own stories and situations set within an established world. Some properties are more rigidly controlled than others. Either way, if you're contracted on a work-for-hire basis, the entity that holds the trademark and/or copyrights to the setting will retain *all rights* to your novel. That means if the novel goes out of print, you have no right to bring it to a different publisher. You have no control over foreign rights, reprint rights, film and television rights—any of that stuff. The licensor/publisher owns it, lock, stock, and barrel, and can do with it what they please—and the overwhelming majority of the time they'll do right by you and your work, making it available for sale wherever they can and for as long as they can.

This is not something open to negotiation. No matter how in-demand an author you may be, you will never own the rights to your Star Wars novel. Some publishers offer flat fees for tie-in work, but most pay advances and royalties just like any traditional publisher.

NOVELIZATIONS

A novelization is a novel that is written directly from someone else's story. You may have read novelizations for movies such as Star Wars. Novelizations of video games are a more recent creation, and in some cases publishers have created novelizations of movies based on comic books. (HarperCollins even published a novelization of the movie *Where the Wild Things Are*, which was itself based on the children's book by Maurice Sendak.)

If you're just starting your career and are offered a novelization, go ahead and do it. There is little risk of "typecasting," and if the movie (or whatever else you're novelizing) is well-received, the pay-off—not just in royalties for that novelization but a subsequent halo effect for the rest of your career—can be substantial. If the movie is a flop, your novelization will probably disappear quickly, too, leaving you free to move on as though nothing ever happened. No one has ever blamed the failure of a major motion picture on the author of the novelization.

Before you start writing, though, get the best, most complete information about the property you're novelizing. Pay close attention to continuity—if you don't and you get the story wrong, a good editor will demand revisions until you get it right. A not-so-good editor will let it just be wrong, then the fans of that property will be harder on you than you might imagine. Novelizations can be fun, an interesting storytelling and writing exercise for both new and established authors, but for goodness sake, please take them seriously.

TIE-INS

These borrow a setting from the source material, and sometimes characters, but the story, even the principal characters, are original to the author.

Borrowing a setting means that quite a bit of that upfront world-building work will have been done for you. If you borrow characters (as you might if writing, say, a Star Trek novel) you've got that as well, so that means less work in the formative stages of the novel. Some authors and readers tend to believe that this makes writing tie-in fiction *easier.* But after fifteen years of direct experience, I can tell you this is not the case.

It's true that you don't have to make up your own rules, but you have to follow—to the *letter*—someone else's rules. Writing good tie-in fiction is as difficult as writing good historical fiction. You can't ignore the "facts," either to satisfy your creative urges or your sense of what's important and what isn't. That means you have to study. The publisher is paying you to write a novel that supports some valuable property, and it's not okay for you to do a slack job.

Editors will—or damn well should—hold you to very high standards, because the fans of the property hold it to those same standards. If you can't bring yourself to care that much about someone else's setting, don't ask to write a book in it. A hot intellectual property like Star Wars or *HALO* is far too valuable to be loaned out to people who don't care.

The Responsibilities of a Tie-in

The author-editor relationship takes on a different cast when you enter the universe of the tie-in. Not only does the editor have the same responsibility to support you, to help make your book and your writing as good as it can be, but he or she also has a duty to the property itself. The owners of a valuable intellectual property are protective of it—and the more successful it is, the more protective of it they will be.

Keep in mind—even when you feel as though you've been dragged into the literary salt mines to suffer over minute details—that if the owners of a property like *Dungeons & Dragons*, *HALO*, or *Star Trek* aren't obsessing over the property's integrity, they're probably doing other stuff to alienate their fans, and all of you are in for a short and miserable literary existence.

If you're being held to setting continuity details, it means your editor cares. There are tie-in books that have sold millions of copies, backlisting for decades. The Dragonlance novel *Dragons of Autumn Twilight* by Margaret Weis and Tracy Hickman, for instance, has been in print continuously for more than twenty-five years. There are tie-ins that are as good as any fantasy or science fiction novel ever written, even if they're often excluded from awards and snobby Ten Best lists.

Veteran author Kevin J. Anderson has written his share of tie-in work. "The advantages and disadvantages both stem from the same thing," he says. "You are handed a familiar universe with familiar characters. I have a running start, in that the readers already know the property; they already love the characters and the situation (otherwise they wouldn't be buying the book). As a fan myself, I get a thrill out of working in and expanding a universe that has meant a great deal to me—*Dune*, Star Wars, *Star Trek*. I can build upon something that is already great.

"But because it is someone else's playground, and because the rules are already established, I don't have the same amount of creative freedom I would have in my own original creation. Sometimes, a story decision that seems obvious and necessary to me is not possible to include because the licensor has other priorities (an action figure design contradicts it, for example). And I don't have the copyright or later control if the licensor wants to build upon what I've added.

"But it sure is a lot of fun."

CHAPTER 35

Move on to Film and Television (If You Can)

I once attended a screenwriting conference in Los Angeles and talked with an agent from one of the major Hollywood agencies. He told me that one of his clients had had a really good day the week before. He'd sold a spec script for a million dollars and got a major studio assignment for another million.

What the agent didn't tell me was how long that writer had been banging his head against the Hollywood system before he had that two-million-dollar day, how many spec scripts he'd sold before that, for how much less money each, and so on.

Hollywood is full of stories about huge paydays, about writers who go from obscure and impoverished to rich and famous in one day. Rumors abound of Hollywood writers who make a million dollars a year and have never had a script produced.

Those stories of huge paydays, however fantastical, have moved a lot of the bad writers from the slush piles of New York publishers into the slush piles of Hollywood agencies. These writers are motivated by the belief that it's easier to get rich in Hollywood now than in New York, and screenplays are "sexier." Some people think they're easier, and they are—kind of. But they are *much* harder to sell.

IN HOLLYWOOD, THE AGENT RULES

There may be book editors who will read your novel even if you don't have an agent, but no serious movie or TV producer will. In the movie and TV business, an agent is essential. Screenwriting is also controlled by a union, the Writers Guild of America, which accounts for why movie and television writers are paid more than non-union novelists. But it also makes the Hollywood writing community more restricted.

There is no shortage of books on how to write and sell a screenplay; refer to their good advice. You may need two agents, one in New York to handle your book deals, and one in Hollywood for movies and television. However, as Brendan Deneen, an agent and the author of the Flash Gordon tie-in novels, explains, "It's most important to have a good publishing agent. If you write a great novel and get it published, the film community will find you."

They'll find you, but they might not hire you. According to Deneen, "Hollywood doesn't really care about novelists, in terms of screenwriting. If you have a good agent and a lot of interest in your book, you might be able to negotiate the first draft (or so) of the adaptation." If not, a screenwriter will be assigned by the studio or production company to adapt your novel, and your involvement with the movie will likely end there.

Deneen recommends you start with a novel before you try your hand at selling a screenplay. He adds, "If you sell your novel, there is a very, very good chance it will actually be published. If your screenplay is optioned, there's still a pretty small chance it will actually get made."

Think of it this way: How many novels are published in the United States every year, and how many movies are released? In 2007, Hollywood released more than 400 movies. That same year, approximately 407,000 books were published—one thousand times as many books as movies. That means you stand a much better chance of publishing your novel than seeing your screenplay turned into a movie.

You may want to try writing your next great idea as a screenplay first. A screenplay is basically an expanded outline with the dialog filled in. Then flesh out the screenplay into a novel. If you end up with both done and ready to show to agents, you'll be covering both bases at once. But study screenwriting before you jump in. Though the basic elements of good storytelling are the same, there are peculiarities to that craft we can't cover here.

CHAPTER 36

JOIN THE ELECTRONIC GAMING REVOLUTION

Over the past few years, more and more fantasy and science fiction authors have gotten day jobs in the video game business. PC- and console-based games are now a bigger business in the United States than the movies. In 2008 the video game business topped $21 billion. That same year, 2008, was a record year for Hollywood, but the movies still brought in less than half that: $9.76 billion. Novelist Jess Lebow, whose video game credits include *Guild Wars*, told me that "there are some freelance opportunities for creative writers in the video game industry, but most companies want to have a team of writers on staff, especially if they are making an online game."

Lebow explains the writer's role in game development: "Initially the writer is responsible for the building of the world and the creation of a narrative outline," he says. "As the process continues, he or she will work with other departments to make sure the characters, environments, and design mechanics mesh with the story being told. As the game takes shape, the responsibility shifts to the generation and editing of text."

As the technology behind games becomes more and more advanced, games will tell increasingly complex and compelling stories. From their narrative-free beginnings in *Pong*, electronic games have advanced to spawn tie-in movies and novels of their own, creating surprisingly rich characters and game play that relies on moving through a story full of plot twists and supporting characters. This flows both ways, too, with a number of electronic games based on movies, or even other games, like the various *Dungeons & Dragons* or *Warhammer 40,000* spin-offs.

THE ADVANTAGES OF HIRING WRITERS

Storytelling in electronic games is still in its infancy. Many studios are starting to realize what a talented writer can bring to the table. They also recognize that writing is a craft, and the fact that you've read books or gone to the movies doesn't make you a writer. Having a talent for coding or 3D modeling doesn't mean you understand what makes a compelling character or an interesting story.

At the moment, the video game business doesn't place too much value on published authors. According to Jess Lebow, "It's still somewhat of a struggle. Some game studios understand the value of good writing. Others not as much. They know that they need text and dialogue, but often they don't fully understand the value of a well-told story. The good news is that this is changing, and that the fans are demanding that their games also have good stories."

That being the case, you could be well served by sending your writing to video game studios—if you're also a fan of video games. Don't try to convince someone that you're the best choice to create a story for a video game if you're not a gamer.

To Sum Up

The publishing business is a tough one. It's sometimes heart-lessly unforgiving, and if you're a new author it will seem closed off—especially when the whole industry is reeling from the recession—but editors and agents are still on the hunt for the next breakout book, and the next breakout author. Are you the next Stephenie Meyer or J. K. Rowling?

Always present yourself like a pro or be prepared to be dismissed as an amateur. Keep your message simple and posi-tive. Don't be overwhelming, needy, angry, or defensive. If you get criticism from an agent or editor, consider yourself lucky. If they really thought you sucked, you'd have gotten a form rejection. If they think enough of your work to give you a tip or two, consider it carefully. Editors can be mistaken, but if you have access to someone's experience and expertise, take advantage of it.

PART IV
HUGO MANN'S
PERFECT SOUL

R. A. Salvatore was kind enough to contribute the following short story, which has never been published before. It is an excellent example of a genre story that is *about something*, as you'll see from Salvatore's comments following the story. Look at it as a good example of the possible range of the genre and for some of Salvatore's tricks of characterization and plotting. Anyone who thinks the fantasy and science fiction genres are all about swords and ray guns hasn't read . . .

Hugo Mann's Perfect Soul

A Short Story by R. A. Salvatore

From the desk of Hugo Mann

By the time you read this, I might be dead.

I say "might," but it's only a question of courage now. I'm certainly convinced that I'd rather be dead, that I'd rather let some unfortunate corporeal entity (or entities, if it gets portioned) take on this perfect soul of mine and face the future that I do not wish to face.

I guess you could call this a suicide note. I prefer to call it an explanation, and if you come to view things the way I have come to view them, and if you are a human being, then you'll not begrudge me the bullet I put in my head. Of course, if you're one of the majority now, one of those who was not so fortunate in the soul-picking game as Hugo Mann, then you'll probably have a good laugh.

I remember looking into the mirror on that morning when all this began, on that first occasion when Richard suggested that I go to see him professionally. I don't often look into the mirror anymore. I like to say that it's because I'm completely comfortable with my appearance, but I suspect that it's more a matter of fearing what I might see. I'm closer to fifty than forty and a million years removed from the playing fields reserved for younger men, but it isn't vanity that keeps me from the mirror. I have little care that my chest seems to have fallen into my waist, even less care for the salt that has invaded my pepper-black hair. I fear what's on the inside, what might be reflected in my blue eyes. They were bluer when I was a kid—hell, my nickname was "Husky Dog"—but the color, the luster, has been slipping away.

I looked that morning, though, brushing a hand through my hair and rubbing it over my face, deciding that the mirror was wrong and I really didn't need a shave.

Vanity.

I was going to college, you see, between jobs and wondering if I could rediscover some of the impossible hopes of youth. There was something exciting about sitting in a classroom again, especially surrounded by beautiful (or at least perky) young, bright-eyed ladies. Someone once told me that the only positive thing about getting older was that more women looked good to you. I'll buy that.

I don't know why I chose to take a class on Mark Twain. Something about that old coot tugs at me, some sense of reality in his writing that always made me think he knew what other people should but didn't. And don't. I understand Mark Twain better now, and I know why he died in bitter misery.

That morning I took my usual seat beside Dr. Richard Hilgedick, a fellow student nearly twice my age, and he gave me his usual smirk and wink. I had been immediately drawn to this guy, on the first day of class—as soon as I realized that he wasn't the professor. The initial attraction, of course, was that he was the only one in the room older than me, which gave me a weird sense of power over the guy, like I could understand the dynamics of the classroom experience better than he.

That lasted until he looked my way and flashed me that disarming grin, that smug—not bad smug, just perfectly content—grin, his properly trimmed gray beard and moustache forming sharp angles around the corners of his mouth. Perfectly content and perfectly proper; the guy had posture that rated eleven on a scale of ten.

The professor, a tired gent maybe ten years older than me, came in soon after. He looked as bored with life as I felt. His hairline started halfway up the front of his head, as though constant stroking by that nervous hand of his had pushed it back to there. He read the attendance right off, pausing, his eyes going wide, before he chanted, "Richard Hilgedick?"

"Right here," Richard answered easily.

Some jock from the back, who should have been out banging rivets with his forehead and not in a college classroom, snickered, and the young lady on the opposite side of Richard couldn't bite back her nervous chuckle. He looked at her, right at her, right *through* her brown eyes, and calmly said, " *'Hilge'* means 'huge.' "

Then he looked back to the front, still perfectly content, while the girl—and she seemed a girl, a lost, little girl, at that moment—turned the color of a McIntosh apple. There had been no malice, no foreplay, in Richard's answer. And while he hadn't said it in a condescending way, I knew that he didn't give a shit about little Miss Perky. It was as if he had looked at her, uttered three words, and let her know in no uncertain terms that she was a puppet, and he held the strings.

It was curious how the girl's clothes no longer seemed to fit her so fashionably, how she suddenly seemed a frightened child in the dressing, make-up, and perfect nails of a college woman.

I was too impressed to laugh at the joke, and Richard soon turned to me, nodding his approval of my approval. He didn't look through me, as he had the girl, and I got the distinct feeling that he saw some substance within me that prevented such a superior scan. I thought it was my age.

Was I wrong.

***

Richard and I became friends right there in that first class, and during the semester we had some of the most outstanding, outrageous discussions of Mark Twain. Often we would linger on the campus hours after the class, talking and arguing, sometimes with the professor, sometimes alone. My wife, to her great credit, accepted my excuses, understood how important this intellectual relationship had become to me. Hell, I think she was just glad to see me excited again, excited about anything.

And it was exciting. Richard was a psychotherapist and had an answer for every question about Twain's ultimate depression, the escalating cynical attitude that haunted and consumed the man until he died.

"I could have shown him the truth of his despair," Richard boasted.

"And that would have made him happier?" I asked with open sarcasm.

"No." It was among the most profound statements I have ever heard, coupled by a look in Richard's brown eyes that broke my heart.

It was at that moment that Richard invited me to come in and see him professionally. I was taken aback—I never thought I needed therapy and wondered what the hell this guy had noticed about me.

"I can show you things that you never expected to see," he said.

"About myself?"

His nod was full of . . . "gravity" is the only word I can think of to properly describe that nod, and the penetrating look in his brown eyes. "And about the others," he finished, as solemnly as a priest at a graveside service.

"*The* others," he'd said. What others? Richard flustered me, scared me even, but I liked him anyway, and I trusted him, so I agreed to go.

I looked in the mirror again on the morning of my appointment with Richard, but I didn't suspect it would be the last time I would see myself in quite the same way.

***

"Past Life Regression Experience." That's what Richard called it, and when he spoke the words, his expression was as straight and as serious as I had ever seen.

"Past life?" I hadn't meant it as a question, really. I was just mulling over the words, trying to decide how far my patience with Richard would go.

I've never been an overly religious man, more concerned with the here and now than with the hereafter and then, and always considered reincarnation as the stuff of bad Shirley MacLaine jokes. I'd never given it a second thought, actually, but Richard had, as was obvious from his trembling hands as he set the single candlestick on the small table between us.

"You can't really expect me—" I began to protest, but he cut me off with a knowing look. He had heard it all before, I realized, countless times.

"What are you afraid of?" he asked, again with that professional calm, that supreme confidence. Suddenly, I knew how the little girl with the perfect clothes in class had felt.

I stammered over the question for some time, not really having an answer.

"If I'm wrong or if I'm right," Richard said easily, "either way, you've learned something about yourself, and about the truth."

"What truth?"

"*The* truth."

I remember bringing my hands up and scratching hard at the back of my neck. I didn't usually do that; there was something very different about this nervous reaction, something tingling. Why was I so anxious?

Richard lit the candle and took out a pocket watch. A pocket watch! I remember thinking how cliché this whole thing was, like a bad movie. I also remember my silent insistence that I was one of those strong-willed people who couldn't possibly be hypnotized. I had seen nightclub hypnotists, and whenever my date suggested I go up to the stage and try it, I would only shrug and say there was no way I could be hypnotized.

I think I was afraid.

I don't remember anything Richard said; I don't remember going out.

Later in Richard's office, he questioned me about my experience. I was lighthearted about the whole thing. I believed that I had dreamed a fairly unremarkable dream. I was a young kid again, running for some reason or another along streets, looking up at the street signs and asking directions. I was frantic, desperate almost, though for the life of me I couldn't remember why.

"Oh, one more thing," I told Richard. "I skidded to a stop at a corner and nearly slipped into the street. You should have seen the face of the driver."

"What driver?"

"The driver of the truck that almost ran me down!" I explained with a light-hearted laugh. I didn't understand.

"What did the truck look like?" Richard asked, and his intensity was amazing.

I shrugged. It was just a truck. "Old," I said. I had a distinct feeling the truck was old.

Richard nodded, again with that smug smile.

"Is there something significant in that?" I asked, and I was quickly growing impatient.

"What was the name of the street?"

I closed my eyes and tried to conjure the memory, but the dream was fast slipping away. Finally I visualized the sign and answered. Richard chuckled.

"Is there something significant?" I asked him again, though I knew by his expression that I had indeed hit on something.

"Was this a memory or a dream?" he asked me.

It was the first time I had thought about it in that manner, and after a moment I just shrugged, at first not understanding what the difference might be. And then it hit me. I understood why Richard had been so interested in the truck, in the street sign. He was thinking that my dream had not been a dream at all and not really a memory either. He was thinking that I had just experienced a moment from a past life.

"When have you been to Germany?" Richard asked in all seriousness.

I had never been out of the country. I started to tell him that—then I realized the street sign was in German.

My wide-eyed expression came as no shock to cool Richard. He reached over and pushed "rewind" on his recorder, stopped it a couple of times, looking for a specific spot in our previous conversation.

"In your recounting, you only related one piece of actual dialogue," he explained. "When you stopped to ask the woman for directions. Do you remember that now?"

I vaguely remembered the incident, but the words escaped me, lost in the fuzz of the fading dream. I was a bit embarrassed, thinking I should make a conscious effort to try to remember some of my dreams in future, maybe even begin writing them down.

Richard started the tape, and for a moment I was truly confused. It was my voice, no doubt about that, but I couldn't understand a damned word I was saying!

The dialogue was in German.

"What does this mean?" I asked Richard, and believe me it was hard for pragmatic Hugo Mann to get those words out of his suddenly dry mouth.

"Go home and think about that question," Richard answered. "I'm not going to try to convince you of anything. But you're going to convince yourself."

***

Richard sent me back several times over the next few weeks. Twice I returned to that youthful time in Germany and learned from a newspaper lying in a gutter that the year was 1938. Also, from a World War II book Richard had, we were able to trace some of the street names I recalled, and we came to believe I was in Berlin.

The whole thing was merely an adventure for me, a game, a play, and while I eagerly fell in with Richard's research, I didn't really believe any of it—at least not any of Richard's claims that I was having a past-life experience. After all, I was born only seven years after the date on the newspaper, and in the dream I was just a kid.

In all seriousness, more grim perhaps than I had ever seen him, Richard reminded me that many kids in Germany in 1938 did not survive the next seven years.

Running through the Berlin streets was only one of my experiences. I was in Italy during the Renaissance. Richard was not the least surprised by that. I sailed the Mediterranean—on a pilgrimage, I believed for some reason I couldn't pinpoint. I hunted a seal in the Arctic along with my Eskimo tribesmen. I worked a field, maybe in the Scottish highlands.

I was a woman that last time, Wordsworth's proverbial "solitary highland lass," and the play was grander indeed. I coyly asked Richard if I might try to get back there, see if I could find a mirror . . . The dirty-minded old lout got a laugh out of that.

Through it all, I was continually amazed at the playback of the tapes. I was speaking languages I had no knowledge of. Hell, when Richard brought the Eskimo tape to a professor at the college who was supposedly versed in Native American languages, he couldn't make out a word of it. He did say, though, that it sounded correct, that the accent and inflections closely corresponded to some of the older tribal Eskimo tongues.

It was starting to get scary, but it was also fun. An adventure, a bit of spice in a settled life. My wife thought I was crazy; my kid thought I was cool.

I thought . . . hell, I didn't even know what I thought at that point. I was in a movie, and Richard was running the projector.

***

"You're going a long way today," he announced on one visit. I was in a good mood that day; we had just received our grades. I remember telling Richard about my A, and he waved it away without regard, as though my announcement was no news to him.

"The only way you couldn't get an A in a Mark Twain class would be if the professor was completely devoid of a soul," he explained. "I looked into our professor's eyes, and I can assure you that he's fairly well-souled."

What the hell was this guy talking about? I shrugged an agreement and let the matter drop, not even wanting to know.

"A long way today," Richard said again as he set the candle on the table, his brown eyes sparkling eagerly in the flickering light. His hand was trembling again, more than I had seen it shake since our very first try.

"How long?" I asked. For some reason, Richard was scaring me.

He shrugged. "I don't think any specific date is important this time," he replied.

I started to question him about that cryptic answer, but he put a finger over pursed lips and promised me that I would come to understand.

***

"The world was bright, the colors vivid. I stretched in front of the rising sun, basking in its glory, absorbing its warmth and energy. I was naked—we were all naked, men and women and children, but we were not even conscious of that fact. It didn't matter.

"All that mattered now was the tall savannah grass and the warm sun.

"And then the world changed."

So did my breathing on the tape. Richard stopped the recorder and looked at me directly.

"How did it change?" he asked. He had never before interrupted a tape playback after a session, but this time it was as if he realized that my memory of the past-life experience remained strong in my mind.

I stumbled for words then shook my head in frustration. I couldn't explain it.

Richard lifted a hand to calm me and started the tape again.

"The sun was gone—like an . . . eclipse, but not an eclipse. We were afraid. I was afraid, but . . . shit, I don't know. It was like something warm came down and touched me, touched all of us."

"Then what happened?" Richard's voice on the tape prompted after a long pause.

"It was different. Just . . . different. The sun came back, and we were still in the grass, still . . . .

"But it was different. Better. Everyone was closer together, and I remember . . . damn, there was more energy between the lot of us than from the sun. We were . . . ."

Richard shut off the recorder and looked at me again.

"What did I see?" I asked.

Richard's wistful smile brought me a great degree of comfort, and I needed it when he gave me his answer.

"Genesis."

"Genesis?" I probably don't need to tell you that my tone showed me to be less than convinced—and I'm sure that you're less than convinced as you read this. And yet, there was a nagging truth to Richard's explanation. A part of me could not deny that I believed him.

Richard went on to explain his theory to me. I'd call it a "wild story," except that I didn't think it wild. I'm still amazed by that.

"There was a moment in human history," Richard declared, "a definite beginning when humanity was separated from the animals, when *Homo sapiens* were given that special spark of conscience and rationale."

"By what?" was the logical question. "By God?"

Richard called it a "collective human soul."

I was more than a little excited by all of this, especially since I'd just witnessed what he was describing. He went on to tell me that I was not his first—he said "client" for lack of a better word, but I felt that he should have said "friend" or even "kin"—who had been at Genesis.

"Were you there?" I asked him.

I knew he had been, and knew, too, at that moment, that his being there was the whole reason he was conducting this research. What Richard was hinting at, what I had felt at that dawn of human history, was something beyond anything this world could offer to me: perfect serenity, the completely religious experience.

It occurred to me as Richard went on that his finding me, finding someone who had been there, even given my growing belief in reincarnation, went against astronomical odds. How many people were there at the dawn of humanity? Certainly not five billion. And since my personal regressions went across racial and gender lines, how could Richard logically rule anyone out?

His pained expression when I asked him that question told me that I wasn't going to get my answer at that time.

"You're going on another trip," he said after we had shared a silent lunch.

"Today?"

Richard nodded.

"Back to Genesis?" I asked hopefully.

Richard shook his head. "Your pilgrimage," he explained. "You're almost there, and I think you should see its end this day."

I started to blurt out a dozen questions, mostly concerning why I had to do it that same day. Regression takes a lot out of you, and I was tired.

But Richard would hear nothing of delays. He promised that my journey would teach me much.

***

"No, I was not on the boat anymore. And I was alone. Maybe this wasn't a pilgrimage."

"Just follow where the memory leads," Richard interrupted, a bit sharply.

"There are timbers all around me, standing. My feet are in sandals. The grass is torn."

My breathing got heavy on the tape. I looked up.

"Not timbers. Crosses."

A long pause.

"Fucking crosses!"

"Where are you?" Richard demanded.

There came a shuffling. I was trying to run out of the room. Richard shut off the tape.

He caught me by the door, just as I was opening it, hit me with a flying tackle that slammed me against the door and sent both of us into a crumpled pile at its base. I squirmed around to face him, to get away from this wild man. And God, his eyes were wild! He scooted to his feet quicker than I could react and shifted so that he was against the closed door, holding it fast.

"Where were you?" he demanded again as I turned on him and backed off a cautious step.

I stared at him, horrified. I thought Genesis was something spectacular, but this was too much for a sheltered Catholic guy from New England.

"Where?" Richard stepped out, grabbed the front of my shirt, and spun, slamming me hard against the door. He wanted to tear the name from my mouth.

I returned his grasp and straightened, pushing him back to arm's length.

"Calvary," I said quietly.

"And what did you see?"

I remember shaking my head back and forth. I remember Richard slapping me hard across my face.

"I saw him," I admitted, and I was crying. I was fucking crying like a baby.

"And what did you see?" Richard asked, suddenly calm. He let go of my shirt and smoothed it with sympathetic hands.

"In his eyes?" he prompted after many seconds slipped past.

"I saw . . . ." What did I see? "It was like those people on the savannah," I tried to explain. I thought I sounded foolish, but Richard nodded eagerly, understanding. I drew strength from that, felt as if I was not alone, and not insane.

"I saw . . . a perfect human soul?" I asked as much as stated, for I really didn't understand what the hell I was talking about.

Richard backed away another step—I could have left the room then, if I'd wanted to. But I didn't want to—and he knew I didn't want to. He smiled, but it wasn't a happy smile. He was sad, and I was, too, though I didn't understand why.

"And perfect human souls were rare, even in that time," Richard remarked as he walked back to the table.

It was the most curious thing I had ever heard. And perhaps the saddest.

So Jesus Christ had a perfect soul. No surprise, right? Of course not. If he had possessed anything less, I would have been surprised.

But what the hell was I talking about? How could I possibly know that Jesus Christ had a perfect soul? What distinction can you find by merely looking into someone's eyes, even if that person just happens to be your savior?

***

I got the shock of my life (and by this point, you can see that's saying quite a bit) the very next day. I went back to Germany, was again that young kid running frantically along the streets.

A young kid running to see his leader.

And I did get a glimpse of that monster as his open-topped car passed along the waving crowd. Adolph Hitler looked right into my eyes.

Right into my eyes.

The son of a bitch. The monster with the perfect human soul.

"It makes no fucking sense!" I later screamed at Richard. "I can almost buy it all. Genesis. Calvary. That's good, that's right. But this guy?"

Richard didn't seem surprised. "There are burdens to possessing a perfect soul," he explained, "burdens that can break the strongest of men."

"What the hell does that mean?" I demanded. "And what does it mean to possess a perfect human soul? Wouldn't we all—"

"No!" His answer sat me back in the chair as surely as if he'd slugged me. That fear flapped up around me again, so many black wings.

"Suppose that it was a finite thing," Richard remarked.

"Suppose that what was a finite thing?" I asked.

"The collective human soul, the spark of Genesis."

"So?"

"How many people do you think were caught in that spark?" Richard asked. "Fifty thousand? A hundred thousand?"

"What difference can that make?" I replied angrily. I really didn't see where his logic was headed.

"How many people are around now?" he asked pointedly, and I couldn't reply, though suddenly I knew the answer. "Suppose that the collective human soul was a finite thing," Richard reiterated. "A finite amount of energy, or whatever it was. It filled the fifty thousand beings, or hundred thousand, or two hundred thousand. Five billion might stretch that a bit far, wouldn't you say?"

The implications stole any forthcoming responses from my mouth. I sat back and stared blankly as Richard elaborated on his theory. "Human beings multiply—physically—of course, but the collective soul is finite. And," Richard assured me, as serious and determined as I'd ever seen him, "that soul is not divided evenly."

"Some have it and some don't?" I asked.

Richard nodded halfheartedly. "Some have it and some don't. Some have a lot and some have a little. It's a random thing, as far as I can tell."

"And we have a lot?" I asked.

"Look at my eyes," Richard implored me, and I did, and I knew that he had a perfect soul. And I knew that if I looked into a mirror, I would see the same spark. I could recognize it now.

"Perfect souls," Richard went on. "You and me. And by the way, if you had none, you couldn't go back to any past lives, because you wouldn't have any past lives. And if you had a little, then you might grab bits and pieces of one previous existence. Or maybe none at all."

It sounded logical; the soul is what remembers, not the body. I could buy that, but still, so many things were out of place.

"What about . . . ?"

"Hitler?" Richard finished, following my trail of doubts. He chuckled and flashed that sad smile once more.

"I've been wondering about that one since I started doing this twenty years ago," he explained. "You can imagine my excitement when we first discovered you were in Berlin before the war."

"He should have no soul!" I declared. "It makes no sense."

"Oh, but it does," Richard assured me.

"So now you're a fucking Nazi?" I wanted to take the stinging words back as soon as I uttered them. Of course Richard was no Nazi; from everything I had seen, the man was truly compassionate and tolerant, if a bit blunt at times. But the image of that murderous butcher with full-souled eyes—any image that put him in the same light as Jesus made me sick to my stomach.

"Hardly," Richard answered, taking no offense. "But I was curious about Hitler. It seems that the most outrageous characters of human history are either perfect or empty. People in the middle— regarding souls, I mean—don't seem to be earth-shakers."

"How could someone as horrible, as repulsive as Hitler have any soul at all?" I asked with conviction. Up to this point, everything I had learned, particularly the revelations on Calvary, reinforced my spiritual and religious beliefs, actually strengthened my faith in God. But I wanted little part of any God that would endorse the monster that was Nazi Germany.

"I told you there were burdens," Richard explained. "Suppose this repulsive person—and I agree with your description—came to recognize as you have, a degree of soul within someone's eyes. He wouldn't understand it, of course, he would simply react to what he saw. Perhaps young Adolph Hitler looked into the eyes of a Jew—"

"So Jews don't have souls?" I asked sarcastically.

"Please!" Richard yelled at me, and he seemed thoroughly disappointed. "Would you please throw away your religious prejudices?"

"You said it, not me!" I argued.

"I am giving you a possible example," Richard retorted. "I already told you that the soul-getting game is a random thing. Religion has nothing to do with it. Race has nothing to do with it. Gender has nothing to do with it."

I put my face in my hands and rubbed hard. I wasn't used to being scolded by Richard; it went against the bond we had forged.

"So if a young Hitler was wronged by a person, and when he looked at this person he recognized the emptiness of soulless eyes, and this person just happened to be a Jew . . . ."

"He might carry that with him forever," I reasoned, and it began to make perfect sense. "In his twisted mind, he might come to instinctively believe that all Jews were bad."

Richard nodded in perfect agreement.

"That doesn't excuse—"

"Absolutely not," Richard strongly agreed. "The man was a beast, a butcher, but I'm not surprised that he was a butcher with a soul. That, I tell you, is what broke him."

"Why?"

"Because he *knew*!" The sheer weight of Richard's heavy tone knocked me back. "Can't you see the implications of what I'm telling you?"

I wasn't sure I could, wasn't sure I wanted to.

"How did you find me?" My question seemed logical enough.

"The same way you were drawn to Calvary in your previous life," Richard answered.

"You were drawn to me?"

"No, not like that." He was chuckling again, and I was glad. This conversation needed a little levity.

"I've found that soul-filled people tend to enjoy Mark Twain," he explained. "I've spotted at least portions of souls in nearly half the people I've encountered in Twain classes, and you're the second perfect soul I've found in one. I'm taking another Twain class, at Sister Diane Community this semester, though I hold no illusions that I'll find another one like us in my lifetime."

"But why Twain?"

"We can relate to the guy, I guess," Richard answered. "I met him once, in a previous life, of course, and can assure you that he had a perfect soul." Richard paused and chuckled again, then looked at me, his expression incredibly sad. "Look where it got him," he said with a helpless—so very helpless—chuckle. "*The Mysterious Stranger* and a bitter end. Some humorist, huh?"

It struck me then how many of the most notable comedic talents wound up dying in despair. Was that profession naturally attractive to people with perfect souls? I guess it made sense. When you can't do anything about something this dark, you might as well fucking laugh about it.

"Where's the other guy you found with the perfect soul?" I had to ask. "Did he find his way back to Genesis?"

Richard nodded. "And I think he was on his way to Calvary, too, but he got killed before we could find out."

"Got killed?"

"In that previous life," Richard explained. "A robber on the road, I suspect."

"Where is he now?"

Richard shrugged. I suspected he was hiding something from me.

***

And I still do. Sitting here now, I suspect that Richard's first perfect soul killed himself. You probably think I'm a ranting lunatic, and I don't blame you if you do. I know that I'd think you one if I hadn't seen these things with my own eyes. I've even considered the possibility that Richard has implanted all of these thoughts into my head during hypnosis.

Except for the recognition. Damn it all. I can look into a person's eyes, any person's eyes, and weigh the degree of soul within him. Any person. And it's gotten to the point where I can't shut this damning talent off. Everybody I see gets measured, and whenever I notice a soulless one, I want nothing more than to run up and punch him in the face, to kill him because I know he is less than human. And I know that we need less people.

All of our hopes and dreams are determined by our beliefs that things are getting better, that mankind is moving in a positive direction. But if the collective human soul is indeed a finite thing (and I know that it is!) then we are moving in exactly the wrong direction. And nothing short of nuclear holocaust or a horrid plague can even begin to bring us back to better days, can even begin to shrink the population so that it is once more in accord with the collective human soul.

I cannot even fathom the many implications. Is it any wonder that, though by any logical measure people are better off now than at any time in our history, the degree of simple happiness is inevitably shrinking? It has to, don't you see, because the level of positive energy, the very spirit of humanity, inevitably diminishes as population expands. No, not diminishes; it just gets spread thinner. Perfect souls were rare even in Jesus' day. If there were two hundred thousand perfect souls at Genesis, there could be no more than one in twenty-five thousand people now! And that's assuming that the souls were distributed evenly. And Richard says they aren't. He says that people like us, like him and me, and that poor bastard he found twenty years ago in a Mark Twain class, are likely one in a million, a number that diminishes with each generation.

And empty people? People without a hint of a soul? "Seventy out of a hundred," Richard insists.

What a burden it is to know this. What a burden it is to see the futility of it all. A "vagrant thought," Mark Twain called us, "a useless thought, a homeless thought, wandering forlorn among the empty eternities."

I think Twain was being kind. Better a vagrant thought, I say, than dying angels.

Still, this is the second draft of my note. The first was strictly an explanation, a cry to anyone who would listen, but certainly not a suicide note. I was interrupted while I was writing that one. A young man's hand tapped my shoulder, accompanied by my son's voice.

"Dad?"

I looked up at him. I looked into the perfectly soulless eyes of my only son.

SOME THOUGHTS ON "HUGO MANN'S PERFECT SOUL"

"Hugo Mann's Perfect Soul" was written in the early 1990s, after R. A. Salvatore had already established himself as the bestselling author of novels like *The Crystal Shard*. The author, who was in his early thirties at the time, explains that he "had met then editor for *Amazing Stories*, Kim Mohan, out at Gen Con, and he mentioned that he wanted to see something from me, and since I had (and still have) tremendous respect for this guy, I wanted to get in his magazine. So I wrote 'Hugo Mann's Perfect Soul,' and was crushed when he rejected it."

A good object lesson right up front. Even bestselling authors don't sell everything to any editor—sorry, Mr. Capote. And rejection can shake the confidence of even a veteran author.

"As a writer, you're always wondering if you know what you think you know," Salvatore continues. "With every work you put out, there are people who take from it something completely different than you intended. You write something you think is great, and it flops. You turn in something you think isn't quite up to speed and see the most amazing reviews for it. So you're always wondering if this will work or if that will work better, or if you have any clue at all about what you're doing.

"So when I turned in 'Hugo Mann's Perfect Soul,' thinking it was quite good, and got summarily rejected (as in, don't even rework it), well, that hit hard. Tempered now in the realities of the writing business, I can laugh about it, of course; it's always hit or miss, with every reader and every editor."

IS IT FANTASY?

The story is an interesting example of the wide range of subject matter—the range of specific execution—that can still fall within the confines of "fantasy," or a broader classification of "speculative fiction," which includes fantasy and science fiction in all their myriad subgenres. But what is it about "Hugo Mann's Perfect Soul" that makes it a "fantasy" story?

"We always tend to get so hung up on labels," Salvatore opines. "Is Star Wars fantasy or science fiction? I see it as fantasy. It hinges on the classic Hero's Quest, and the Force always seemed more magical to me than physiological (thanks for the midi-chlorians there, guys . . .). I think I'm not alone, and that was part of the blow-back when the Force was suddenly 'explained.'

"As for 'Hugo Mann's Perfect Soul,' well, it's got enough mysticism, theology, and suspension of disbelief in it to qualify as speculative fiction, or fantasy, or speculative theology, or whatever else you want to call it."

To Salvatore, "it's simply another look at human nature, which is what I do in all of my books. My purpose in writing is, and always has been, to study the spiritual side of what makes us who we are. That's why I spend as much time in the heads of our villains as our heroes, why I'm as fascinated by [The Legend of Drizzt assassin-villain] Artemis Entreri as I am about Drizzt Do'Urden."

This touches back to what we discussed in Chapter 5. Salvatore had something to say in this story, and he used the freedom allowed by speculative fiction—we could call it *magic realism* and not be too far off—to explore that idea to some depth.

FATE OR CHOICE?

Salvatore continues, "What I tried to get at in 'Hugo Mann's Perfect Soul' was the question of fate versus choice, as much as anything else. Well, in this case, it was a matter of choices made within the characters' predetermined fate—more predetermined, even, than that of a dark elf born in Menzoberranzan. In a way, this story is anathema to the themes I often explore in my later novels, because it infers the deity role in the characters; you're either born with a perfect, or even substantial, soul or you're not, after all.

"Maybe that's why Hugo Mann was driven mad. Maybe the concept of that which he discovered was too discordant for him to accept, or maybe it was too discordant for his god [the writer] to accept it, so I took decisive action."

It's interesting to hear that the author has seemingly been puzzled by his own story. This certainly doesn't mean he wasn't thinking about it. A not-uncommon response from authors when asked about their characters' choices is that the characters seemed to make their own decisions, taking the author along for the ride. Though there is a bit of hyperbole there, there's also more than a grain of truth. Part of what any author does, as I've stressed over and over, is ask questions of the characters. If the characters come to life, as they should, they provide answers—or more questions.

Find the Continuing Themes

It is also common for an author to ask similar or even the very same question from novel to novel, story to story. "Hugo Mann's Perfect Soul" touches on themes common throughout Salvatore's body of work, though perhaps less overtly.

Though this story speaks openly of God and Jesus, in The Legend of Drizzt, Salvatore purposely avoids the invented deities of the Forgotten Realms setting. "I don't want to deal with them," he explains. "When the dark elf Drizzt finds his goddess, it's not that there's some actual being (though in Realmslore, there is) out there ready to help him, but rather, he is introduced to the tenets of the followers of this goddess and finds that those tenets are reflective of that which is already in his heart."

He adds, "From Drizzt's point of view"—like that of Richard Hilgedick's—"it's all choice. There is no predetermined fate. There is no controlling hand playing us like marionettes. I doubt Drizzt would even accept psychotherapeutic notions of being trapped by your childhood experiences—though in more than one instance, he found that he had erred precisely because of that childhood. Still, in the end, he overcame that baggage and made the correct choice before him." In much the same way, Richard (unlike Hugo) can be sanguine about the similarities between Jesus and Hitler: Jesus made better choices.

These ideas, in slightly different ways, went on to inform Salvatore's later work.

EXPLORING THE NATURE OF EVIL

"All of the themes from The Legend of Drizzt carried into Demon-Wars in terms of self-discipline and climbing through station into greatness," says Salvatore. "But looking back now, the thesis of 'Hugo Mann's Perfect Soul' could be applied to DemonWars. For example, those with perfect souls in the short story can carry out acts of great evil, but only because they think they're doing right. In DemonWars, the character of Marcalo De'Unnero is exactly like that. I get more letters saying, 'I hate that guy,' regarding De'Unnero than anyone else, even Artemis Entreri. That monk is one of my favorite characters ever, precisely because he believes with all his heart and soul that he's doing great good, that his means are justified by the end he will bring forth."

The Villain's Motivation

Hugo Mann's inability to reconcile the good acts of Jesus with the evils of Hitler brings us back to the question of a villain's motivation that we explored in Chapter 10. Remember that an unmotivated villain is neither scary nor interesting.

Salvatore notes that when writing DemonWars he "didn't intend any analogies to some of the things we saw post–9/11 in the United States, obviously, since the DemonWars series was written almost in full before that tragedy, but I was making a general statement about my view of human nature. A villain who wakes up every day think-ing, 'What evil can I do today?' is boring. A villain who wakes up every day and simply doesn't care whether he does good or evil, and just does what's best for him, is rather inane. But a villain who thinks himself a hero, a villain who believes that the evil he is doing is for the best, is a villain worth reading about."

WHAT HAS CHANGED?

And now that almost twenty years has passed since Salvatore wrote the story—almost that long since he last read it—how have his ideas and attitudes changed?

"I hadn't thought of the story in a long time when I pulled it out for this project. To my surprise, I didn't cringe when I read it, as is often the case with some long-ago work. In fact, I find myself want-ing to rework the story to punch up the theme even more, and per-haps less obviously. Suppose there is this one meta-being, Human, who lends pieces of his soul to his corporeal manifestations and now that those corporeal manifestations, people, have multiplied so greatly, there's simply not enough 'soul' to go around."

KEEP REVISING AND REVISING

There's something we didn't talk much about: When do you stop revising? If the story hasn't been published yet, go ahead and keep tinkering. Perhaps the ideas behind the story are strong, but you need a whole different way of expressing them.

For Salvatore this may have been the case with DemonWars, a project he regards as deeply personal and returned to several times in his writing life. You will likely also end up with a story that sits in a box somewhere, silently informing the rest of your career.

NEVER FEAR

I hope that over the course of this book I've given you new tools you can use not only to write a science fiction or fantasy novel, but also to do it well. Keep at it and learn from your successes and failures. And no matter what I tell you, what anyone else tells you, *don't give up*.

"If someone can talk you out of being a writer, you're not a writer," screenwriter Josh Olson wrote in an article for the *Village Voice*. If you want to be a writer, keep writing. As long as you're writing, reading, researching, working, revising—even when it feels as though you're just beating your head against the wall—you're getting better.

Remember, Yoda told Luke Skywalker, "Do, or do not. There is no try." He knows what he's talking about.

Write, or write not.

—PHILIP ATHANS
Washington State, December 2009

JOIN ME IN THANKING . . .

This book wouldn't have been a sixteenth as good without the generosity of sixteen people who were like angels on my shoulder:

Lou Anders
Kevin J. Anderson
John Betancourt
Terry Brooks
Brendan Deneen
Ethan Ellenberg
Harlan Ellison
Paul S. Kemp
Jess Lebow
Kuo-Yu Liang
Logan Masterson
J. M. McDermott
Paul Park
Mike Resnick
R. A. Salvatore
Paul Witcover

With a special thanks to Peter Archer for suggesting I do it in the first place, and for being a far more patient editor than I would have been; Bill Slavicsek and Bill Rose for their blessings; R. A. Salvatore (again) for agreeing to be more deeply involved in the whole thing than first he bargained for; everyone on the blogosphere who's visited Fantasy Author's Handbook (*http://fantasyhandbook.wordpress.com*); and as always, Deanne and the kids.

INDEX